MIRAGE IN T

Ejnar Mikkelsen and Ernest de Koven Leffingwell forty-five years after their search for the unknown land north of Alaska.

Mirage in the Arctic

The Astounding 1907 Mikkelsen Expedition

EJNAR MIKKELSEN

Introduction by
LAWRENCE MILLMAN

THE LYONS PRESS
Guilford, Connecticut
An imprint of the Globe Pequot Press

First published in Great Britain

First Lyons Press paperback edition, 2005

The Lyons Press is an imprint of The Globe Pequot Press.

10 9 8 7 6 5 4 3 2 1

Printed in the United States of America

ISBN 1-59228-671-2

Library of Congress Cataloging-in-Publication Data is available on file.

CONTENTS

ILLUSTRATIONS

MIRAGE IN THE ARCTIC

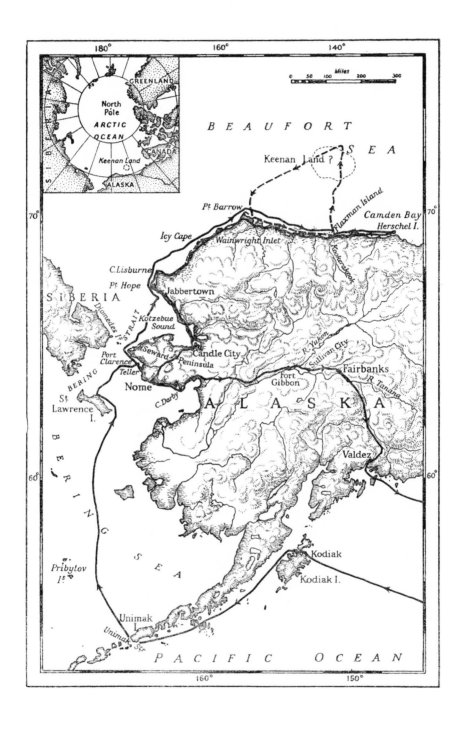

INTRODUCTION

IN 1897, a sixteen-year-old Danish sailor decided to join Salomon Andree's balloon expedition to the North Pole, so he hiked from Stockholm to Andree's house in Goteborg, Sweden, a distance of 320 miles. The sailor, whose name was Ejnar Mikkelsen, already seemed to be taking the same path he would take in his later travels—the path of most resistance.

Andree scoffed at the idea of a mere youth joining his expedition and gave Mikkelsen money for a rail trip home. But what might have been a slap in the face turned out to be a godsend, since Andree's balloon, the *Eagle*, subsequently disappeared off the face of the earth. Thirty-three years later, a Norwegian sealing captain found the freeze-dried bodies of Andree and his companions on White Island near Spitzbergen.

Mikkelsen was nothing if not persistent, and after Andree's rebuke, he tried to become a member of Baron Eduard von Toll's fossil-collecting expedition to the New Siberia Islands. "You are not a scientist," he was told, "and likewise you're too young." This turned out to be another godsend, because most of the expedition, including Baron von Toll himself, ended up vanishing without a trace.

The high attrition rate among Arctic explorers seems not to have worried Mikkelsen. Indeed, he found himself challenged by the prospect of visiting such a potentially dangerous realm. So now he tried to enlist with Georg Amdrup's Carlsberg Fund Expedition to the uncharted coast between Angmagssalik and Scoresby Sound in East Greenland. An earlier expedition led by the Frenchman Jules de Blosseville had attempted to explore this same section of coast, and neither de Blosseville nor any of his eighty-two men were ever heard from again.

This time Mikkelsen's persistence paid off, and in 1901 he went to East Greenland as a member of Amdrup's expedition. The trip featured a harrowing 500-mile open boat journey in ice-filled seas. It also had some tense moments when Amdrup and his men were accused of murdering thirty-eight Eskimoes who, it turned out, had starved to death. But nobody disappeared or even suffered a serious mishap.

"Once bitten, twice shy" is a saying that applies to a lot of things, but not to the Arctic. Those who've been bitten by the Arctic bug seek to be bitten again and again. Mikkelsen himself was bitten even before he traveled North, and after the trip with Amdrup, the bite never healed.

Next, he signed on as a cartographer with the Baldwin-Ziegler Expedition. If anything could have cured his Arctic fever, it would have been this expedition, whose motto was "To the North Pole or Burst." Whatever could go wrong did go wrong: dogs were washed overboard, walruses sank one of the boats, sledges fell apart, and brawls broke out among the crew.

The leader, Evelyn Baldwin, seemed to regard Arctic exploration as an opportunity to get drunk; rather than attempt the Pole, he would retreat to his cabin and drink himself silly, with the result that the expedition seldom left its base camp in Siberia's Franz Josef Land.

"Baffled, Not Beaten" was Mikkelsen's own slogan for this fiasco. He found a sympathetic spirit in an American named Ernest Leffingwell, the expedition's head scientist, and the two became so inseparable that they were referred to as "the Siamese Twins." At the same time they were polar opposites (so to speak). Whereas Mikkelsen was headstrong, impetuous, and romantic, Leffingwell— as perhaps befits a geologist—was as imperturbable as a rock (Arctic exploration, he later wrote, was "just another job").

The two men remained in contact after they got back from Franz Josef Land. Having heard stories of a large unknown land or maybe even a continent north of Alaska, they fixed on the same idea: they would mount an expedition in search of what might or might not be a fiction. For there's no word in an explorer's lexicon more compelling than "unknown."

In that same lexicon, there is no word more profane than "fundraising." Hustling and clawing, Mikkelsen and Leffingwell managed to get funding from, among other parties, Leffingwell's father, Alexander Graham Bell, the Royal Geographic Society, and

4

John D. Rockefeller. But they still could not afford to put a motor on their expedition ship, an antique schooner that had seen action variously as a pearler, an opium smuggler, and a seal poacher. The ship's checkered reputation caused Mikkelsen to ignore an old sailor's superstition: you're courting disaster if you change the name of your ship. Mikkelsen changed his ship's name from the *Beatrice* to the *Duchess of Bedford.*

On May 20, 1906, the sixty-six-ton ship left the port of Victoria on Vancouver Island and began to leak almost immediately. Then when the explorers reached Alaska, their entire crew tried to desert for the goldfields of Nome. In addition, it became increasingly difficult to maneuver the *Duchess* around sea-ice without a motor—so difficult, in fact, that they couldn't reach Herschel Island, the main commercial entrepot of the Western Arctic and the place where they'd planned to overwinter. Instead, they had to settle for Flaxman Island, a barren vastness inhabited by a handful of Eskimoes.

At this point you might think that the Anglo-American Polar Expedition, as it was called, was becoming another Baldwin-Ziegler Expedition. But Mikkelsen was at his best when the odds were most against him. He and Leffingwell became friendly with the local Inupiak Eskimoes (Mikkelsen would later write a novel, *Frozen Justice*, about Eskimo life), and from these denizens of the Far North, they learned various survival skills that would be of vital importance during their forthcoming trip.

In March 1907, they finally headed north to search for the mystery land, accompanied by the Norwegian Storker Storkerson, the only reliable member of their crew. It wasn't long before they encountered, in Mikkelsen's phrase, "a hell of ice." With each passing day, that hell became more and more hellish. Mikkelsen's description of it in *Mirage in the Arctic* is superb: not only do you feel you're there, but also that you definitely don't want to be there. I might add that he's far more adept at portraying nasty ice conditions than his polar contemporaries Shackleton and Amundsen. He was a considerably better writer, too.

Forty years later Mikkelsen and Leffingwell were vindicated when a 350-square-mile ice island was discovered just beyond their "farthest north." Almost as rare as hens' teeth, such islands are the only stable surfaces in a moving, crumbling ice pack, and this one—later known as "T3"—became the site of the first U.S. scientific station in the Arctic Ocean. But the two explorers wouldn't have found it in 1907; an ice island generally can't be located without an airplane, and airplanes were then in their infancy.

If they hadn't returned to Flaxman Island when they did, they doubtless would have ended up in the same Arctic abyss as Baron von Toll and de Blosseville. Yet their troubles weren't over, for the *Duchess* had been crushed by the ice in their absence. Just the sort of thing you can expect when you change the name of your ship.

Undaunted, Leffingwell stayed in Alaska for several more years and made a geological survey of the area now known as the North Slope. This survey turned out to be much more significant than he could have imagined at the time. For its report of petroleum seepages near Point Barrow paved the way for Atlantic-Richfield's discovery of the 9.6-billion-barrel Prudhoe Bay oil field in 1968, not to mention the subsequent discovery of oil in the Arctic National Wildlife Refuge. If Leffingwell had lived a more few years (he died in 1971), he could have joined the debate over drilling for oil in ANWR's coastal plain.

As for Mikkelsen himself, he was not the sort of person who could derive much satisfaction from the relatively sedentary work of a field geologist, so he decided to leave Alaska. Typically, he did this in the most arduous manner possible, by dogsled and on foot, via Point Barrow, Nome, and Fairbanks to the port of Valdez.

Mikkelsen's description of his 2,500-mile journey in *Mirage in the Arctic* has a rollicking, novelistic quality: now our hero has a hairsbreadth escape from a rising tide, now he's entrusted with a $40,000 bag of gold, now he finds the frozen corpses of some prospectors, and now he meets a proverbial pistol-packin' mama. Such incidents almost make you forget that his epic trip was scarcely less demanding than a traverse of the Greenland Ice Cap or a crossing of the Sahara.

His devil-may-care attitude toward danger suggests an Indiana Jones of the Arctic. And like his Hollywood counterpart, Mikkelsen felt most at home when he was farthest from home. As he once wrote: "What are you to do when you are born with eternal unrest in your soul and are drawn only to those parts of the world that sensible people regard as fit only for fools?" The answer is simple—you ignore those sensible people and light out for the Territory.

So in June 1909, hardly a year after his remarkable Alaskan journey, he traveled to his old stomping-ground of East Greenland in another woefully inadequate boat, a single-masted sloop called the *Alabama*. His goal: to find a pair of presumably dead explorers, Mylius Erichson and Hoeg Hagen, along with their valuable maps of the northeast coast.

Once again, Mikkelsen was a magnet for disaster. He got scurvy, nearly starved to death, suffered frostbite, fell into a crevasse, and had his journal eaten by a polar bear. He and his expedition mate Ivar Iversen, a man with virtually no Arctic experience (when he saw his first musk ox, Iversen thought it was a cow), were forced to live in a box of a cabin that was periodically jostled by hungry bears. Stuck in this cabin and seemingly without hope of rescue, they avoided boredom by eating copious amounts of porridge before going to sleep at night. The porridge gave them vivid dreams, which in turn gave them something to talk about the next day.

Two Against the Ice, the book Mikkelsen wrote about the so-called Alabama Expedition, is another riproaring Arctic narrative. Like *Mirage in the Arctic*, it has a "you are there" immediacy that makes it seem quite contemporary (both books originally appeared in the early 1950s); and like the earlier book, it's often very funny, as in the scene where Mikkelsen and Iversen, suffering from an advanced case of cabin fever, get into a heated argument over the merits of their respective fantasy women. No doubt Mikkelsen's ability to see humor even in the most desperate of circumstances helped him triumph over those circumstances.

You might think that Mikkelsen would have had enough of Greenland by now. Quite the contrary. As he grew older, he returned repeatedly to that capacious island's East Coast, although as a champion of the Eskimo cause rather than an explorer. He did not want East Greenlanders to become like most of the Inupiat he'd met in Alaska, a people living uneasily between their own culture and the ascendant culture of White Man. So in his capacity as Danish Inspector General for East Greenland, a position he held from 1934 to 1950, he did everything he could to keep White Man's influence minimal. Perhaps this is one reason why East Greenlanders are among the healthiest and most traditional of Eskimoan peoples today.

Ejnar Mikkelsen died on May 1, 1971 at the age of ninety-one. His longevity poses an interesting question: Who is the wiser, the prudent ones or those who drink the whole cup?

Lawrence Millman
Cambridge, Massachusetts
June 2005

CHAPTER I

THE DIFFICULTIES OF STARTING AN EXPEDITION

The unknown land in the Beaufort Sea—What the whalers and Eskimoes had seen north of Alaska—The apathy of the rich

EVERYTHING seems so easy and straightforward when you are young and a born optimist, and when your mind is filled with exciting plans which you will risk much—no, everything, to carry out.

Naturally, in your youthful arrogance you imagine that you are being thoroughly realistic and practical and have carefully considered all the difficulties which could conceivably obstruct the road to your goal. One way or another these difficulties become so small or—in imagination—so easy to overcome, the elements of uncertainty so unimportant, that the impetuous course of your thoughts towards the great goal is not impeded by anything so humdrum as the possibility of encountering obstacles. They, of course, can easily be dealt with when they come, if they ever do.

So it was in 1905 with my plans to find the unknown land which theoretically existed in the ice far to the north of Alaska.

The first and greatest unknown was of course the question whether this land I had never seen even existed. Time after time I went through all the arguments advanced, all the alleged proofs of the existence of that unknown land, and to me they seemed most plausible. In my opinion there were really no grounds for doubting that the land was there in the Arctic Ocean—quite the contrary. The land must be there, since two ships' crews had definitely stated that they had seen distant mountains rising high above the great masses of ice of the Beaufort Sea, far north of Camden Bay.

But all the same there was a tiny doubt. Could you put any reliance in a report of this kind coming from whalers, people who have had so many strange experiences on the high seas and related

9

so many strange occurrences, that even sailors themselves some-times doubt their veracity? And they were the source here. And then there was the awkward fact that though I had made an exten-sive search in the old annals, both in Europe and America, I had not been able to find out anything about the ship or what the crew had seen—except that it was land which was marked on the maps to the north of Point Barrow and that it was called Keenan Land.

The claim was thus so to speak anonymous, for who was Mr Keenan? It can be dangerous to build too much on assertions of that kind.

There could perhaps have been reason to doubt this evidence had it not been for the other eye witnesses: the officers and crew of *Plover* who on a bright summer's day in 1875 had seen high land rising above the uneven pack-ice off Camden Bay.

This discovery of land, where previously it had been believed there was an immense wilderness of ice, naturally did not pass unnoticed: that distinguished and very cautious body the Royal Geographical Society printed in its famous publication Captain Sherard Osborne's account of what he and his entire crew had seen from *Plover's* deck.

Could you wish for more definite proof of the unknown land's existence? Could you doubt this confirmatory account coming from the numerous, well-trained crew of a naval vessel? Hardly. To me this seemed incontrovertible proof of the land's existence which must remove the last vestiges of doubt. And yet there was still further proof.

Captain Osborne told in amplification of his sensational dis-covery, that in the Beaufort Sea they had found pack-ice of a kind which had not before been seen in any polar waters: improbably massive, often grounded in a hundred feet of water, with high ice hills and deep broad valleys, presumably formed by three of Nature's most irresistible forces in conjunction: frost, snow and the melting action of the sunshine of the short summer. In addition there was the tenacious and incessant pressure of a strong eastward flowing sea current; and to the combination of these was attributed the curious type of pack-ice in the Beaufort Sea, which Sherard Osborne called palaeocrystic ice. And he put forward the theory that this immensely massive and characteristic mass of pack-ice could only have been formed by the current having held the ice packed together year after year, enclosed in an immense gulf between the north coast of Alaska and the south coast of some large undiscovered land far to the north—the land, the highest mountains of which he had glimpsed on that day of quivering sunlight north of Camden Bay.

All this was evidence which apparently removed the question of land or not on the other side of that wilderness of ice from a doubtful supposition far into the world of reality.

Of course there was land there beyond the pack-ice!

The Eskimoes on the north coast of Alaska also knew of the land in the North and had often seen its tall mountains there when the air was sparklingly clear and conditions good. And in the long winter evenings when storm and weather kept them shut in their little huts, their imaginations reached out across the ice to this land which they held to be the objective of the immense flocks of ducks and geese, which every year in the early summer winged their way across the low sandbanks at Point Barrow heading north-east, always north-east, towards the land up there where no doubt they found secure nesting places in sunlit valleys.

And they had a story of how one of them, a great and daring traveller, about whom was an aura of romance, had ventured out on to the ice from Point Barrow and, all by himself, had defied the hazards and difficulties of the pack-ice, and in the end had come to that land. On the outward journey he had followed the path of the migrant birds north-eastwards, and when autumn came he had followed the hosts of them on their southward flight and so returned to his wondering fellows, who had long since given up hope of ever seeing him again. He told a strange tale of the land out there: that game of all kind abounded both in the sea and on land and in the air; that the Eskimoes caught so much and lived in such luxury, that all their women had attained the tribe's ideal of the acme of beauty: which was to be so fat that they were almost bursting, and so greasy that they glistened in the sunlight.

This lone man's feat was known to all the Eskimoes of the coast, and many of the young men talked big about how they were going to do the same and become just as famous—and every time a hunter disappeared out on the ice it added fresh life to the legend: he had gone north, they said, to the land out there with its wealth of game, to the fat women, to a life of freedom from care, of pleasure and belching satiety.

Of course I would gladly have believed every word of the Eskimoes' story about that mysterious land, but I was enough of a realist not to believe more than that the Eskimoes actually had seen land—as all the white men along the coast of Alaska maintained that they had.

In 1900 the discussion was raised on to a different plane when a scientist came forward with what almost amounted to scientific proof of the existence of land north of Alaska. A certain Dr R. A. Harries, who had been studying currents and tides along the coast of Alaska, had come to the conclusion that there must be land on the far side of that wilderness of ice. And he even went further and said: There is land! for he thought he had evidence enough to enable him to draw its position on the map.

One day I received a pamphlet from America, published by the Hydrographic Institute in Washington. That pamphlet confirmed my belief in the existence of the land, for attached to it was a map of the Beaufort Sea and on it was marked a large island some 250 miles north of the known coastline. The map was even so detailed that it showed a long promontory stretching westwards to the longitude of Point Barrow.

Harries' assertion and argument were widely discussed in scientific circles in America and England. Some contested it most violently, but others ardently supported it. And I, well I naturally was firmly convinced that there really was land which you would find if you could only sledge far enough across the appalling pack-ice. And equally naturally it had to be I who found it.

That side of the question was thus clear and straightforward. The land was there. Now, quietly and with an easy mind I could set about the uncertain business of collecting money for an expedition across the pack-ice of the Beaufort Sea to the land beyond, which I had made up my mind I was going to discover.

Even here—despite previous unfortunate experience—my optimism was so stentorian that it quite drowned the voice of doubt. It must be possible to get this money, preferably of course from Denmark, but as Sherard Osborne was an Englishman, England would also do. And if England failed, there was still America, which really ought to have had the greatest interest in the land being found—and where, by all accounts, there were so many rich people.

Nor was it such a dreadfully large sum I was after: forty, perhaps fifty, thousand Danish crowns. That was nothing. Among Denmark's almost three million there must be at least fifty people prepared to give one thousand crowns each for so worthy an object, some perhaps even twice as much, those specially interested naturally still more: in my moments of extreme optimism I all but assumed the money was already lying in the bank.

My search for fifty backers proved a painful peregrination from one rich man to the next, and it did not take long before I realized that if they had thought me an irresponsible fanatic when I had tried to get money to start whaling some years before, their opinion of me now was considerably worse. As a rule the only answer I received to my request for money was a resigned and very eloquent shake of the head—the rich in fact were mostly so shocked at the stupidity of my going to them for a contribution towards an expedition to Alaska that they were almost bereft of speech.

Only one man, Carl Aller, the owner and editor of *Familie-Journalen*, spared the time to hear me out, and he alone had a thousand crowns to give—and I had thought that fifty people would have.

I had to abandon the idea of raising the money in Denmark. The next place to try was of course England, where there were supposed to be quite a number of rich people, and they were, after all, Sherard Osborne's fellow countrymen, and so perhaps for that reason would support an expedition to the land he had seen. But how should I set about it?

A lucky chance came to my help.

I had for some time been corresponding with the President of the Royal Geographical Society, Sir Clements Markham, about my plans to which he had lent a ready ear. A good number of years before he had himself written a paper on the possible, in his opinion highly probable, existence of the land. Now Sir Clements wrote to say that he was coming to Denmark for his summer holidays and suggesting that we should meet at Bellevue where we could discuss the unknown land in peace and comfort—and the possibility of getting the money to go there, if we came to the conclusions that the evidence of its existence seemed sufficiently definite to make the attempt.

To him, then, I took my troubles and for the first time found sympathy and understanding. He had himself been through very much the same in his younger days, and he knew how hard continual refusal can strike.

'I know it,' said Sir Clements, 'I know it. You get so tired and dispirited going from one to the other, explaining to reluctant ears what seems to be so obvious—and then in the end being refused. Yes, I know it all. But you get hardened gradually; I did and so will you. And we must always remember that even though it is highly unpleasant to go to a man and ask for money, it isn't for ourselves we do it, but for the cause. And then it isn't so difficult any more.' Then came the words for which I had hardly dared hope. 'Come to England, my young friend. There you will have the full support of the Royal Geographical Society. We will help you as far as we can, and perhaps you will have better luck with people there than here.'

I did not need to be asked twice. I borrowed some money so that I could go, and one day in October 1905 I found myself in London and thought: What do I do now?

I had Sir Clements to back me up and received more than willing assistance from the Secretary of the Royal Geographical Society, Dr Scott-Keltie, who gave me a list of people who might possibly be interested in the plan and prepared to give money to such an adventure north of Alaska.

And then I also had a magnificent trump which would probably open many doors to me: a letter of introduction to Queen Alexandra from Prince Valdemar of Denmark who had been interested in the plan by his adjutant and friend, G. C. Amdrup, who had been my Chief on my first Greenland Expedition. This letter, however, was only to be used as a last resort, if all else failed. I had given a solemn promise on that score, and I kept it through many difficulties. But the knowledge that I had this great trump was a real stay and support.

And so I went on as I had begun in Denmark: going to see people who could give money to the expedition if only I was allowed to talk long enough to get them interested. And that wasn't so easy, to a certain extent more difficult than in Denmark. I was only twenty-five, a bit awkward and self-conscious, not particularly well-dressed, and my English could have been better. The sailor in me stood out a mile, in dress, manner and language, so that when I had finally forced some door and been ushered in to the man with whom I wanted to speak, I would still be aware of the butler's disapproving gaze and of his thinly veiled displeasure that so queer a person as I should have dared push my way into his house.

That was a most unpleasant sensation, and it acted like oil on a stormy sea, stifling my eloquence and damping my eagerness. After that it didn't require much opposition to make me stop explaining things as I really wanted and just blurt out a request for money, after which I would be accompanied to the door by an arrogantly smiling butler, as penniless as when I came in.

Then suddenly the outlook brightened. My sister and I had gone to London together, for she wanted to try and get in contact with an English publisher so as to obtain English books to translate, and she happened to know C. A. Bang, who was one of the leading lights in the English publishing house of William Heinemann and also a Dane.

After my sister had gone back to Denmark and I had moved for reasons of economy from the relatively good hotel in which we had stayed to a cheap boarding house in Bedford Square, Bang and I saw quite a lot of each other. One day he asked me to come to the office. Mr Heinemann wanted to see me—and perhaps, but only very much perhaps, he would support the expedition by purchasing the right to publish the story of it—and pay in advance.

That made pleasant hearing and judge of my delight when, after making enquiries of the Royal Geographical Society and various other quarters, Heinemann agreed to give £600 for the right to publish everything about the expedition, whether in the form of books, newspaper articles, magazine articles, or pictures, everything—absolutely everything, except possible scientific publications which Heinemann did not consider reading for rational beings.

I realized that Heinemann was a smart business man, and he certainly was not giving too much for the story of the expedition— if we found the land; and as far as I could see his only risk was that we should perish on the way. But even then he should be able to get quite a lot out of telegrams and that sort of thing. The conditions were hard, and when I put my name to the contract I knew I was fettering myself in a way which I was bound to regret often enough in the future, but that was the first money I had got for the expedition and I had to pay the price.

To have money in the bank was a wonderful feeling for an insolvent man. I straightened my back and felt my self-confidence return.

CHAPTER II

THE HUNT FOR 150,000 CROWNS

*Queen Alexandra—I lecture to the Royal Geographical Society and the
results—How I lost the Queen's favour—the Duchess of Bedford—I try
the rich men of America—President Theodore Roosevelt interested*

In my joy at getting the first money for the expedition I let it slip
out in an unguarded moment that I had a letter of introduction
to Queen Alexandra. Heinemann, of course, was interested and
made it quite clear what it would mean to my efforts to get more
money if the Danish princess, whom the English loved so well as
their queen, would agree to be patroness of the expedition. All this
I could easily imagine for myself, and as I was still having great
difficulty in gaining admittance to the world of Society and the
Rich, I wrote to Prince Valdemar and asked if I might make use
of the letter now that the expedition was to a certain extent
assured by the £600 I had had from Heinemann.

The answer was that I might. I received a summons, and so one
day I found myself at the palace. I had gradually acquired such
self-confidence that I took not the least notice of the appraising
looks of the servants.

The Queen, however, was herself a Dane abroad, and she
greeted her young countryman with a friendly, understanding
smile, whatever she may have thought of my youthful enthusiasm
and eagerness when I began explaining why, how and wherefore
—which I found considerably easier to do in Danish than in
English.

The audience did not last long, yet long enough for the Queen
to agree to become patroness of the expedition—but she smilingly
had to regret her inability to attend the meeting of the Royal
Geographical Society at which, some evenings later, I was to present my plan to the committee of that famous body and as many
of its members as turned up.

I had been looking forward to that evening with high hopes and considerable apprehension. It would not be at all easy for me to give an intelligible account of what was known about that undiscovered land and how I thought I and my companion on this, and a previous expedition, Ernest de K. Leffingwell, were going to reach it.

Inevitably the evening came. Every seat in the lecture room was occupied and, while I sat mentally recasting my little speech for the umpteenth time so as to present my case as convincingly as possible, I was aware of the voice of an Englishman giving an eloquent account of his recently concluded expedition to some distant part of the world.

To my infinite relief and delight I was spared having to explain the reasons why there should be this undiscovered land to the north of Alaska, for old Sir Clements himself stood up and said what there was to be said both for and against—but mostly for, as he himself believed in its existence.

There was considerable applause when Sir Clements wound up by announcing that Her Majesty the Queen had consented to be patroness of her fellow countryman's expedition to this unknown land and that the committee of the Royal Geographical Society had decided to give it both moral and financial support. Then, without any transition, came the words I was so dreading: 'Mr Mikkelsen!'

It was not easy for a young man whose inadequate English called for a certain benevolence in the listener, suddenly to find himself on his hind legs looking out over row upon row of pale faces on which there was no apparent sympathy or understanding to be read, just the indulgent waiting, the same disheartening expression I knew so well from the faces of those to whom I had gone for money when they had already made up their minds not to give a penny.

It was not stimulating; and it was those pale unfeeling faces I now had to thank for the moral and financial support they were giving to the expedition, and then try to explain how we would set about finding the land I had just been given money to discover.

This last was almost the worst of all, for my plan was still very vague, since so much depended on the amount of money we received. Every additional thousand crowns in the bank altered our plans to some extent, and I was already busy planning to buy a ship. It was thus by no means easy to explain that this was how we would do it if we didn't get any more money than we had at that moment, but that we would do this and this if a kindly fate should bring us, for example, double or treble that amount.

Really only one thing was definite: the aim of the expedition, which was the land away there in the North. That we were going to find—unless we had to be content with determining where the edge of the continental shelf lay and so the limits of the continent —the land's end.

For the first time my somewhat peculiar English proved a help, for my audience did not understand a great deal, and that was quite a good thing. But they were friendly and afterwards there was a discussion of the project and the plan—or as much of it as they had understood. One and all approved of the idea, including a sharp-eyed, tall, slender man who spoke English with so strong a Norwegian accent that even I could hear it. This was Fridjof Nansen, and afterwards, in a language more natural to us both, he wished me luck and success and promised to support me where he could—and this he did, amongst other things by writing an article for *The Times* warmly commending the expedition.

After the meeting a bearded man came up to me, talked about the expedition and ended by inviting me to go and see him somewhere, only where I had not understood, on a day which I also didn't gather. He must have told me his name, but I didn't hear that either in all the babble there was. Luckily Scott-Keltie was standing near, and when the tall bearded man had vanished in the throng, which was not easy, as he took up as much room as a bear, I asked Scott-Keltie who, where and when?

Scott-Keltie laughed: 'You've a lot to learn yet,' he said. 'That was Rothschild. He is very rich, very interested and has his own zoological museum at Tring—you must pay some attention to him. If he felt like it, he could easily finance the whole thing himself.'

Well, he didn't do that, but he gave something towards it and not so little either, and all he wanted in return was the skin of a Kodiak bear. That was easy to promise, for we were intending to touch at Kodiak Island anyway, and no doubt would meet bears enough.

The next morning brought a lot of journalists to my modest room in Bedford Square to talk about my plans and all that sort of thing. The last of them was a man from *The Morning Post*. He was as young as I; he had travelled quite a bit, read more and knew what he was talking about. We got on together like a house on fire, talked a lot about many things, and then suddenly he put his finger right on the crux of the whole thing: 'Tell me,' he said, 'how on earth are you going to sledge so far across the ice? You'll never be able to carry enough dog food!'

Correct, said I, glad he had thought of that, for I had worked out a solution which I myself thought rather clever, to say the least of it, and which I was not loth to make public. Here was an opportunity, and so I told him: each dog could pull a hundred pounds from the start of the sledging, and when a hundred pounds of food had been eaten, one dog became superfluous from that point of view; so we were going to shoot the worst dog, cut it up and feed it to the other dogs, thus saving at least a couple of days' dog food for every dog which became superfluous.

'Brilliant idea,' said my new friend, and off he went—and the next morning there was a long interview in *The Morning Post* which included that bit about the dogs. I was very well pleased. An interview like that must surely bring in quite a lot for the expedition's already shrunken funds.

The reaction, however, was not what I had expected: a summons from the Queen to go there at once!

I expected—yes, what actually did I expect? I don't know, only not what I found: the Queen with *The Morning Post* in her hand

and a severe look in her eyes which had been friendly and smiling so short a time before. 'Is this story about the dogs really true?' she asked.

Yes, it was true enough; for otherwise we should never get far enough into the ice with a dog team unless we happened to come across game.

'That I can understand,' said the Queen, 'but I am patroness of the Society for the Prevention of Cruelty to Animals and you will realize that, however much I should like to help you as my fellow-countryman, I cannot give my patronage to an undertaking where dogs may be treated as you perhaps will be forced to treat yours.'

That was a shock. Things had been going so well and everything had been so promising, and now a fuss over the dogs!

My face must have revealed something of what I was feeling, for before the end of the audience the Queen had promised me another patron who was not on the RSPCA and thus not so particular: Mary, Duchess of Bedford, an exceedingly wealthy, very helpful and widely-travelled woman, who had sailed her own yacht to Jan Mayen Island and had musk oxen running loose in her great park. That sounded well, and it proved even better when the Duchess invited me for the weekend to Woburn Abbey.

There were a whole lot of guests, people who had apparently never been hard up. They were also familiar with their surroundings; they all knew each other and spoke a language I scarcely understood, for there was not a great deal in common between their English and that a young sailor acquires as he knocks about the world, so that there were surprises on both sides.

It wasn't at all easy there, and although the Duchess tried to make me feel at home, I couldn't help feeling like a fish out of water—and naturally I was not dressed like the others, how could I have been? Also I looked in horror at the host of servants who, though condescending to me, would certainly expect a bob or two when I left. But whom I should have to tip and how much, that I had no idea; surely I couldn't tip that distinguished-looking butler?

Even this difficulty was overcome, as difficulties always are. In this case the Duchess called me aside and told me that such and such of the servants, including the butler, should have so and so much. It was an appalling list and the total more than I had on me; but the Duchess was obviously prepared for that too: 'Here you are, young man,' said she and put the money in my hand, to my very great relief.

The Duchess introduced me to a number of her friends, and some let themselves be induced to give money for the expedition, though perhaps not so many or so much as I had expected and hoped—yet it was enough together with what my companion, Ernest de K. Leffingwell's father had promised, to let me feel that the expedition now had sufficient financial backing for me to go to Norway and order sledges and polar equipment and to buy sledge provisions and such things in Copenhagen.

On the way to America I stopped in London in the hope of getting a little more money, for I had unfortunately already begun to find that what I had bought was proving much more expensive than I had calculated. Few had any comfort for me. In America, said those who ought to know, shaking their heads, it will be much worse still. They know how to pile it on there.

So I just had to arm myself as well as I could, and put my trust in a perhaps vain hope that the Americans would be better than their reputation.

I paid another visit to Woburn Abbey to thank the Duchess for her help and all she had done. This time I no longer felt such a total outsider as I had before, for I had a top hat to help bolster up my self-confidence—and luckily there was nothing to show that the duchess had sent it to me, apologizing that people in England were still so narrow-minded that such a monstrosity was necessary if you were to get on with the servants. That at least was what she wrote, but perhaps there were others as well who thought you ought to wear such a hat. Anyway, now I had one—and that was a great moral support.

On my last evening in London the committee of the Royal Geographical Society held one of the customary dinners which in the more carefree past always preceded one of the society's evening meetings, and to which all distinguished travellers who happened to be in London were invited. There were many guests, all in evening dress, and each of them represented a distant and little known land or country. And they spoke of the things they had seen and experienced without big words—just the right company for a young traveller to be in.

Then the President rose and gave the traditional toast: 'Health and success to all travellers abroad!' And each of those present stood up and repeated the President's words: 'Health and success . . .' while their thoughts went out to places where bold friends were trying to explore Nature's secrets in unknown lands.

And then there happened something for which I was quite unprepared. In front of each diner was a brass bowl and a tiny glass which the waiters now filled with champagne, only a thimbleful. Then the President stood up, looked up and down the table, nodded to me and said: 'Mikkelsen!' 'Mikkelsen' repeated all the others, rising and draining the few drops of champagne in their glasses—which they then knocked on the brass bowls so that they smashed with a tinkling sound.

There must have been a look of amazement on my face, for Scott-Keltie laughed and, leaning forward across the table, explained: 'That's a custom we have had since 1785 when we acquired these bowls. There are only a hundred of them, so there mustn't be more than a hundred people present when they are to be used. And whenever a man sets out on an expedition which has the support of the Royal Geographical Society and he can eat his last dinner together with us, we put out the bowls and those little glasses which we have just smashed, because they must never be used again once we have drunk from them and wished the departing one God speed wherever his path may lead.'

Behind me stood a bowing waiter with a salver on which lay an envelope: 'With the compliments of the Royal Geographical Society and the best of wishes.' and when I opened the envelope there inside was a cheque for £200.

Since then I have been given a lot of money for expeditions and such like, but never in such a handsome and traditional way as that gift from the Royal Geographical Society in February 1906.

At the end of February I found myself in the midst of the hubbub of New York. The Royal Geographical Society had advised me to seek the help of the American Geographical Society, and there I went, met the Secretary, smiling, kindly Dr Adams and asked him: 'What do I do now?'

Luckily Dr Adams was *au fait* with the situation, for the Royal Geographical Society had written to tell him that I wanted more money and expected to be able to get it in America. They had also said that it was only right and reasonable that America should pay a share of the costs of the expedition, both because it was an American who had recently provided the theoretical evidence for the presence of land there beyond the ice-horizon, and because it would have to become American territory—if it did exist and was found.

That was also what Adams thought, and luckily he personally believed in the existence of land in the Beaufort Sea. As he also knew Dr Harries he was ready at once to help with word and deed, not slowly and with due regard for procedure as were the English, but as an old friend who slapped me on the back and promised friendship and support. He was calling me by my Christian name by the time we had spent a quarter of an hour in each other's company; he telephoned right and left, dictated letters to influential people, swept like a storm through the office getting the staff busy with this or that, all to help me as best he could. And this was the America where evil tongues had prophesied I should encounter nothing but grief and trouble!

When I left Dr Adams that evening I had in my pocket a long list of names of those I should go and see. To some of these intended victims Adams had already written, he had spoken with others on the telephone. Some names had red ticks against them—these were the probably certain givers—others had a question mark: 'These are the ones,' explained Dr Adams, 'who have money and who have previously given to this sort of thing. But whether or not you can get anything out of them will depend entirely upon the mood they are in—if you can ever get in to see them.'

And so I began another hunt for money in new surroundings, with new methods and different victims.

The really big capitalists were too rich for it to be possible just to walk in and see them. They barricaded themselves behind a host of secretaries and managers, each of whom in turn had to have explained to him what I wanted of the rich man. They were friendly enough, but they didn't let me in. Of course, they would tell the rich man what it was I wanted, and also they would let me know if he intended to give anything. But that day, unfortunately, it was not possible to get hold of him: he was engaged, he had gone away, was ill, dying perhaps, any excuse was good enough and the secretaries used them unblushingly, as long as they thought they would damp my ardour and keep me from coming again.

I never got in to one of the really rich, and, though it must be an expensive business surrounding yourself with so many people, I can see that the employment of endless subordinates and inquisitive secretaries pays hand over fist. They are there to keep the money seekers away from the rich man, and they have a fantastic ability to drain a poor wretch of the last vestiges of hope.

It was, I suppose, pretty naïve of me to try and get to see John D. Rockefeller or the railway king, Harriman; but I had been told that they were the richest men in the world who could and should give something—and I had still not yet made the acquaintance of the wonderful defences surrounding these Croesuses. The attempt was an utter failure, in fact only once did I manage to speak to one of the really rich and that was Graham Bell, inventor of the telephone and lots more, a multi-millionaire in dollars.

I had tried to see him at his office, where of course I was fobbed off with pretty phrases and smiles. By then I was growing tired of vain knocking at office doors, and so decided to take the bull by the horns and go to see him in the bosom of his family where presumably he wasn't surrounded by secretaries. When I came to

Graham Bell's house, which was in Baltimore, lights were blazing in all the windows and there were a good many of those! Hosts of people were coming and going, most of them in evening-dress, but there were also some not much better dressed than I.

So in I went following the stream and eventually I landed in front of the tall, powerfully built man with a huge white beard, whom I knew to be Graham Bell from the pictures you saw of him everywhere. He looked enquiringly at me, and so I began to tell him what I was trying to do and what I thought he might and ought to do.

He looked quite taken aback, and in fact said that he was, but he also told me to come and see him at his office the following day. I didn't feel like doing that, for I knew what would happen, and I told him so without mincing my words. And he, the gruff old man, laughed: 'Are you afraid they won't let you in?' he said. Then he wrote a few words on a visiting card: 'Just show them that, and it will be all right.'

Then I was invited to join the party, and Graham Bell's daughter seemed to think I was a droll character, for she kept with me all the time, introduced me to lots of people, talking and laughing, and was sweet and amusing—and the next morning I went blithely to the office, showed my talisman and, lo and behold! the barricade of secretaries, managers and directors opened and I found myself in front of Graham Bell. 'What was it I wanted?' So then I explained and he gave something, not such a lot as I had expected of that very rich man, but all the same—yes, it was definitely worth all the trouble I had taken to see Graham Bell.

My pushfulness must certainly have made an impression, for when I met his daughter again nearly fifty years later, she could still remember her father's astonishment at my—should it be called cheek?

I had been told that President Theodore Roosevelt was very interested in Arctic exploration and had given Peary a lot of support, so perhaps there was a chance that he would back me as well, if not with money, then with concessions and favours; there was so much an American President could do to further and help a young man with strange plans. Robert G. Peary whom I had met two or three times had been friendly—it was not his Pole I was after—and he had advised me to see the President. The Danish Minister in Washington prepared the way with a letter, and one day there I stood, confused, in front of the President: I had never dreamed it would be so easy and hadn't really thought out what I actually wanted of him.

But it was all right. The President must have found out before-hand what the American Geographical Society thought about the undiscovered land beyond the ice-horizon north of Alaska, and he was interested. He gave permission for the Revenue Cutters in all waters where I might be to be instructed to help me, and he promised that my equipment from Denmark and Norway should pass through America unopened and without the Customs making a fuss. There were other things as well, but I have forgotten them now; all that remains is the memory of a very virile, strong-looking man with sharp eyes behind heavy glasses, a man who wanted to know quite a lot of things and who asked my opinion about the fiasco of the Baldwin Expedition in 1902—and of the unknown land there in the north.

CHAPTER III

THE OUTLOOK BRIGHTENS

*Russia comes to my help—I buy a ship—Hectic days in Victoria, BC—
Money pains again—The telegraph does the rest*

My visit to the President was only a short one, but it had quite considerable repercussions. Some journalists took it into their heads to report that I had promised the President to take possession of the as yet undiscovered land for America, and this was one of the stories telegraphed on the subject to Russia. The reaction there was apparently rather violent. *Novaja Vremja* demanded that the Russian government should immediately intervene, and *Journal de St Petersbourg* clamoured for the despatch of a torpedo boat or two to watch for me in the Bering Strait and protest on behalf of the Tsar against my taking possession of the land for America.

There was quite a fuss: it sounded almost as though there were going to be a war about land whose existence had yet to be proved. However, the war didn't come that time, nor did I see any torpedo boats in the Bering Strait when I came there some months later in a peaceful little schooner which was certainly not intended to stand up to warships.

Stupid as the Russian fuss was, it provided me with a welcome 'open sesame,' for many doors which had remained closed to the young arctic explorer were opened wide to the hero of the Russo-American squabble about the land which had yet to be discovered.

In Washington I met R. A. Harries, the man who had delineated in theory the land I was to try to find. He was head of the Hydrographic Department in the Ministry of Marine, a small, shrunken figure. He was quite frightened by all the commotion his unknown land had aroused; every mention of 'Harries Land' in the papers made him squirm, and he was horribly afraid lest he should prove to be the indirect cause of my companions and

28

myself suffering hurt and hardship, perhaps even losing our lives in the attempt to find it.

It was painful to be with him, the quiet scholar, for he kept on and on explaining and going through his calculations to convince himself and me that they were correct. How he could be bothered! After all, he had been young himself once and he must have realized that no young man would worry whether his calculations were correct or not, once he had got it into his head that the land was there and that he was the one who was going to find it.

There was nothing to be done about it, nothing at all, and poor Harries was almost in tears when I said goodbye to him for the last time: 'Take care, friend Mikkelsen, for heaven's sake take care!' And as the train began to move, he called out after me: 'I believe the land is there; I spent all night working through . . .' I didn't hear the rest, but I knew what he must have said : '. . . . my calculations again, and they are correct all right.'

New York brought a handsome addition to the expedition's exchequer: I received contributions from Danish friends, the Carnegie Foundation and various Americans—even Harries gave from the little he had; in fact it all went very well.

One morning I found on my table a letter from the American Geographical Society and out of it I pulled a cheque for an amount which was a very pleasant surprise. I could not help thinking, however, of that dinner in London at which the Committee and members of the Royal Geographical Society had wished me Godspeed with a mouthful of champagne; the smashed glasses and the tradition and solemnity of it all. And now this: a formal letter, a relatively large cheque and a receipt form attached.

The language was the same, more or less, the people the same, more or less, but the difference in the way things were done, seemingly so small as it was, cried to high heaven of a new people, great and rich, yet lacking something of that which sheds sunshine and warmth over the greater poverty of life in the old world.

A few days later I left New York with about eight thousand dollars more in my pocket than when I arrived. That was a lot of money, and I ought to have been jubilant, yet I wasn't. New York had confirmed a nagging fear which had been tormenting me for some time: all prices in America were sky-high compared with what we were accustomed to in Europe. And yet I was told that it would grow much worse with every mile I travelled West. And I was to travel thousands of miles.

I met Leffingwell in Chicago. Leffingwell and I had been together on an expedition in 1902, and we had liked each other so well that we had decided to do something together. And now we were. He was cheerful and had every reason to be so, for his father, who was owner and head of a famous—and expensive—boarding school for pampered daughters of the American money-aristocracy, had given him ten thousand dollars as his contribution to the expedition.

We discussed our finances, Leffingwell and I, went over estimates and prices, added and subtracted and came to the joyful conclusion that we ought to have money enough, and even to spare. Bursting with plans and zeal I hurried on across the endless prairie, across the Rocky Mountains, and down to the Pacific Coast.

Swiftly as I had travelled, the telegraph had been quicker still and every owner of every little ship on the Pacific Coast had obviously heard about the crazy Dane who was looking for a ship for some idiotic expedition to the Beaufort Sea. If you were stupid enough to want to get up an expedition to find an unknown land far out in a wilderness of ice, instead of making money like other Christian folk, looking for gold in Alaska for example, if you had to have excitement and danger in your life, you didn't deserve anything better than to be cheated right and left.

That's what the owners of small ships thought, and very much what several people said to me when a proposed deal went all wrong. The result was the inevitable one: from the moment I looked at the first ship on the Pacific Coast the prices of all little ships rose and rose with every day that passed.

In Victoria BC I at last found the ship of my dreams: a splendid little schooner with tall slender masts and a rig which promised well for speed and spread of canvas. But unfortunately she had no auxiliary motor. But did that matter so much? The expeditions to the polar regions in the olden days had managed with sail alone, and the whalers had practised their dangerous trade in large sailing ships which on the whole had acquitted themselves well among the ice of the Arctic Ocean, and we moderns—this was in 1906—were certainly just as good seamen as they.

In 1906 it was a comparatively new thing to have motors in ships. They were not particularly reliable, but very expensive, and so I refused the many offers made me to install one, though I always let the manufacturers know that if they would present us with a motor for the sake of the advertisement, we would gratefully accept it. But buy one? No, we didn't have the money for that.

Our ship had had a very adventurous and chequered career before we bought her for the expedition. The story was that once many years before she had been a Japanese naval vessel which had gone ashore in a storm. The wreck was then bought by someone or other who must have been a very clever shipbuilder, for of the timbers, which consisted of teak, camphor wood and other tropical woods, he built in 1879 a lovely little schooner of sixty-six tons, which was then used as a mother-ship for poachers hunting the precious fur seals among the Pribylov Islands in the Bering Strait. That only lasted until, inevitably, the schooner became too well known and had to stop her highly illegal but most lucrative occupation. She then took to pearl-fishing in the warm and presumably also forbidden waters of the tropics; some years after that she had become so notorious in the little ports of the East as an opium smuggler, that an English gunboat was sent to look for her —and, when the crew discovered that the game was up at last, they cold-bloodedly ran her ashore and abandoned her to her fate, though the cargo of opium mysteriously vanished with them.

A Canadian bought her next, got her afloat, repaired her and once more equipped her for sealing, but this time it was entirely legal, so he insisted. Evil tongues, however, said that there wasn't a great deal of respectability or legality, and there must have been something at least in the talk, for the ship could not show herself as a sealer in the Bering Strait without risking confiscation if she were captured by either Americans or Russians.

Friends suggested that I might perhaps be able to get her cheaper because of this, but I had no luck there. Her owner was a hard-boiled business man and in no particular need of money; at least he himself said that he had made quite a nice bit out of the sealing as long as it lasted.

Time, however, was getting on; the Polar Seas would soon be open to shipping and we could not wait. So the ex-naval vessel, ex-pearler, ex-opium-smuggler, ex-seal-poacher became a respectable exploration ship with an exciting future ahead of her.

She had to be thoroughly overhauled; the rigging and sails were gone over and partly renewed; there was much more to be done to the old ship than I had expected and, of course, it was also far, far more expensive.

Once again I began to be worried by lack of money, or rather by the fear of it; for though I suspected that everything I had had done on the Pacific Coast would be expensive, I was careful not to tot it all up and see how dicky our finances really were. That, however, was brought home to me one day when I was having dinner at the Union Club. A man came across to my table, a man I knew well, the manager of the bank which had our money, a friendly man, a cheery chap who usually had a joke for you when he met you.

But he didn't look at all jocular as he sat down at my table and, after a word or two about the weather and such like, he suddenly said: 'Tell me, do you realize that today you have overdrawn your account in the bank?'

I didn't rightly know what 'overdrawn' meant, for it was quite a new thing for me to have an account at all, but it was obvious from his serious expression that something was wrong. 'No,' said I, trying to dismiss the matter, 'I didn't, but that will be all right.'

'Yes,' said the bank manager, 'we shan't quarrel about the

hundred dollars you owe the bank; but—tell me: how much do you owe other people here?'

I tried to get out of answering that very awkward question, but the man just produced a piece of paper and pencil: 'Now, skipper,' said he, 'no more nonsense. You know well enough things are bad; so out with it.'

There was no avoiding it: I had to face the facts and realized that the next half hour was not going to be pleasant, for I had kept sufficient track of affairs to know that I owed far more than I could pay.

But how much? That was what we now had to find out. I began enumerating all the things I had bought but not yet paid for, while he wrote it all down growing graver and graver and once or twice giving his head a shake: 'Any more?'

When there were no more, he drew a line underneath a long column of figures, added it up, whistled and looked across at me: 'Yes, you're well and truly in it. Do you really not know how much you have to find before you can take the boat out of harbour?'

I did have some idea, but not that the amount was as large as it actually was. There was over twelve thousand dollars to be found before we could sail—and our account in the bank was overdrawn. It wasn't a pretty prospect, and the bank manager obviously didn't like the look of it either when he asked the question I was expecting: 'What are you going to do about it?'

That was what I didn't know, but after a sleepless night I went to the bank and got hold of the manager: 'Listen, will you as a private person lend me a few hundred dollars?'

He naturally thought I had taken leave of my senses, but when he had pulled himself together and we had discussed my idea a bit, he laughed and said: 'All right; I don't think it will come off, but, like you, I'll take a chance and risk the money—and good luck to you!'

After that I went to the telegraph office and sent off a sheaf of telegrams to people all over America and England, people whom

I had previously tried to see but had found my way barred by a smiling army of secretaries, people who already had given something, and also to those of whom I only knew that they were supposed to be as rich as Croesus.

The telegrams were almost identical, they explained that the expedition had stranded on the dangerous rocks of insufficient funds and urgently asked the recipient to telegraph something to help refloat it so that it could get started before it was too late in the season.

It was, of course, rank optimism to expect any favourable result from such an appeal, but it really was my only, however slender, hope, and I shut my mind to any thought which could have been interpreted as doubt—for that was too heavy to bear.

Two days after I had sent the telegrams the bank manager came up to me beaming and waving a telegram: 'From Rockefeller,' he said, and there was veneration in his voice:

TELL MIKKELSEN FIVE THOUSAND DOLLARS TRANSFERRED AS IMPUDENCE REWARD

I didn't let the snub worry me; I was too delighted and also surprised. Leffingwell's father also provided more of the coveted dollars than he had given before, and four days later I was able to meet all my obligations. My friend the bank manager and I celebrated the joyful event with a little dinner in Union Club. It was a good dinner, and a merry one, but of course he was right when he said, smiling: 'Well, skipper, it came off—but it shouldn't have!'

It was, too, high time that we got away from these eternal worries about money. Summer was approaching; the roses were already out in lovely Victoria and the time when we should have to leave rapidly drawing nearer. Yet there still remained a lot to do and to arrange, including money yet again—for of course we had nothing over with which to pay the crew's wages at the end of the voyage.

Once again we were up against it, but things turned out better than we expected or deserved, for the young men who were prepared to go north with us were not thinking so much about money as about the adventure and—as it turned out—the gold diggings in Alaska. We were to touch at several places there, and in those days Alaska was attracting as many of the adventurous as could find space in a ship.

Thus matters were arranged comparatively easily in that we pledged the ship against the wages the crew would be due to be paid in a year or two's time, and a lawyer drew up an imposing-looking document according to which I undertook to sell the ship within eight days of our return; but in the event of the ship not coming back—as was by no means unthinkable, then the men lost their wages. It took good people to accept such conditions for wages they were to earn in the sweat of their brow; but then we were going to the land of gold and it was perhaps as much that fact as the wages which attracted them.

And then there was the question of the ship herself. She was called *Beatrice* when I bought her, but she had had her name changed before when she had become too notorious on her devious ways, and could have it done again. You can't go out exploring in a ship called *Beatrice*.

It was the Duchess of Bedford who had given us the start which made the expedition more or less financially assured, as well as no small sum of her own money, so it was only natural that we should want to honour her by renaming our ship *Duchess of Bedford*. All Victoria's upper ten were invited aboard for the ceremony which was performed by the Vice-Governor's daughter and ended with a ball in the club—not at the expedition's expense, but at that of the Vice-Governor who took the opportunity to present us with a welcome cheque from the Government of Canada.

Being a Dane I was not allowed to command a Canadian vessel as *Duchess of Bedford* was, nor own her, and to have transferred her under the Danish flag would have been so lengthy and complicated a business that the idea had to be abandoned at once. As the law also forbade the sale of a Canadian ship to the USA it was not even possible to have Leffingwell as the owner; so we hit upon the idea

35

of asking the Duchess of Bedford to be the formal owner of *Duchess of Bedford* and charter her to me for six shillings a year, which would allow me to command her and satisfy the law in letter and spirit.

Telegrams flashed between our little *Duchess of Bedford* and Her Grace herself in the splendours of Woburn Abbey. The Duchess agreed and the legal formalities were arranged; the ship was loaded, the crew signed on, and we were able to clear for 'the unknown land in Beaufort Sea' with myself as skipper. At last the day of departure had arrived, by the morning all the difficulties—and they had been many—would be things of the past and forgotten, but it had been hard while it lasted.

In the early morning of 20 May 1906 we hoisted sail and watched expectantly for the first faint signs of the morning breeze which would take us out to sea.

It came, but at the same moment we caught sight of the Harbour Master's little steam launch obviously making for us and wondered what was wrong now. The launch came alongside as we were getting the anchor up—and in her bows stood our last creditor in Victoria, a spluttering, wrathful Chinese tailor whom we had had press our trousers the evening before so that we could look more or less presentable for our last evening in civilization—and whom I feared we must have forgotten to pay the dollar or so he was due for his pains.

My presentiment was correct as far as I could understand the agitated little yellow man's English, and I hastily sent one of my companions round everyone aboard to see if together we could scrape up the dollar or two the poor Chinaman had so honourably earned. But no, we didn't have it; twenty cents was all the ship could manage.

With the anchor up and wind in the sails *Duchess of Bedford* slid slowly ahead followed by the Harbour Master's launch and the screeching Chinaman.

Near us lay an Admiralty inspection ship, HMS *Shearwater*. The skipper and officers were friends of ours, and not the people to fail a comrade in distress. So I held down towards *Shearwater's* stern where the crew stood lined up to bid us a fitting goodbye—and as we came within earshot I shouted across to the skipper asking him to free us from the persecution of the vociferous Chinaman by giving him the couple of dollars he was demanding.

Captain Hodgson laughed and nodded. 'What, still in financial straits?' he shouted, and a couple of silver coins glinted in the sunlight. The Chinaman fell silent, and while *Shearwater's* crew cheered us on our way, her siren howling and her flag dipped, we eased off the sheets and steered towards the open sea. The voyage had begun in earnest.

In the years which followed I completely forgot *Shearwater's* skipper and the readiness with which he had paid our debt to that angry Chinaman, but some thirty years later I happened to give a lecture one evening in the Royal Geographical Society, and afterwards an elderly white-haired admiral came up to me, shook hands and after a little talk, said: 'Do you remember the Chinaman in Esquimalt Roads?'

'The Chinaman?' I looked at him blankly.

He laughed. 'Perhaps you don't remember *Shearwater* and the skipper who got you out of a slight hole? That was me.'

Then I remembered it all, the departure from Victoria, the Chinaman and the dollars, so the next day I gave him lunch.

CHAPTER IV

FAIR WEATHER AND STORM

North through the Pacific—Kodiak Island—Problems in the Bering Sea—
Missionaries and Traders—Gold hunger and its consequences—
Port Clarence

It was a relief to be able to turn our backs on all the worries we had had in lovely Victoria and stand out down Juan de Fuca Strait with a fair wind that made our little *Duchess of Bedford* dance across the wavelets glistening in the sunlight on her way out towards Cape Flattery where began the open sea, the all but endless Pacific Ocean.

Astern lay all the tedious business of finding money and the worry of making as sensible and responsible use of it as we were able—though others no doubt considered we had been most irresponsible in what we had done.

Ahead of us lay the adventure we had so long been dreaming of, and even though it would most certainly cost us dear in toil, labour and privations, it was more man's work than going to people cap-in-hand for money; now, as we tried to carry through our undertaking, we had only ourselves to rely on.

That worried us not at all, on the contrary, we welcomed it after all those months of living under the yoke of money and of having to rely on others to give us enough of it.

Now we were as free of all such cares as the gulls which flashed like chalky lightning low above the tops of the masts, screeching their delight at being alive. Now we would be sailing, living life to the full; let the squalls of rain come now, no matter how violent, and wash all the dust off our bodies and souls which life ashore with all its problems has deposited on and in us. Life seemed glorious indeed as, with spray at her bows and a seething wake astern, our little schooner headed out towards the endless sea with falls hauled tight and sails billowing in the fresh breeze.

Glorious is perhaps too big a word to use about life on board, for in the days, weeks, months and years which lay ahead we were not altogether free from care and worry. But at least we did not have money worries and that was something to be glad of. We had come to be fairly easily satisfied in our pleasures.

But what worries?

Well, yes, nothing less than that the *Duchess* began to leak really badly as soon as we got out into the restless Pacific. We had certainly not expected that, and of course we ought to have steered straight for the nearest land to find the leak and have it repaired.

We didn't do so, however, for several good reasons, though one was more than sufficient in itself: we didn't have the money to pay for even the smallest repair, in fact we didn't have any money at all on board, nor any credit on shore. So we remained at sea and pumped the clear sea water out of the ship at every change of watch, steering our course as well as we could, and rejoicing that the *Duchess* scarcely leaked at all when we were on the starboard tack. As long as the wind showed consideration it wasn't so bad; otherwise we just had to try to trim her so that the leak let in the least quantity of water.

It was, of course, bad enough having a leaking ship in the midst of the expanse of ocean, but we comforted ourselves with the thought that things would improve in a couple of months or so, when we got into calmer water among the drifting ice floes. Until then we just had to keep the pump going. And we had a magnificent pump on board, so big and good that it ought to have aroused my suspicions when I bought her: you don't put so efficient a pump as that into a ship without good reason; so the leak must have been an old one, and the seller had known of it!

But that didn't make it any less of a leak.

Lord Rothschild had given money towards the expedition and in return had asked for the skin of a Kodiak bear for his zoological museum at Tring. So, since Kodiak Island lay on our route we put in one fine day to that wild, tall island in the hope of being able to satisfy his wish—and at the same time have a bit of a rest from the everlasting pumping which in the long run becomes very tiring.

We made an honourable attempt to get the bear whose skin I had sold for a good round sum, but after some days' scrambling about the mountains and glens we had to give up. We saw plenty of tracks of the great beasts, and the natives even brought us the skin of one they had just shot; but for some strange reason or other they had cut the head off the skin, so nothing came of that deal. It was another proof of the rightness of the old saying that you shouldn't sell the skin till you've shot the bear.

Thus Lord Rothschild did not get his bear skin, but even so our consciences were clear when we broke anchor and steered out from the lovely, mirror-surfaced fjord towards the restless waters of the Pacific—back to our pumping.

Those were difficult waters we came to next. White-capped breakers fringed dangerous rocks wherever we looked, or shot up like troops of tall white ghosts above the black sea, easy enough to avoid by day, more difficult at night, when they were only visible by the phosphorescence glowing in the mighty cascades which could suddenly rise up like gleaming but deceitful beacons right in our course.

However, it is the sailor's lot to live dangerously when he sails in waters that are not well known. And any way the risks you run are always worse in retrospect. When you are in the midst of rocks and can hear the roar and tumult of the breakers and see pillars of fire shooting upwards into the night, you have no time to think of dangers imminent or otherwise. Our every nerve was stretched as we tried to sail clear of unknown and unseen rocks, and fear and irresolution had to wait till we lay in safer waters.

It was nerve-racking sailing until we reached Unimak Strait, the gateway to the Bering Sea, which is flanked to the west by Unimak, a black island riven by violent volcanic outbursts, and to the east by a volcano almost ten thousand feet high, a perfect cone round whose base the surf of the Pacific Ocean and the Bering Sea rages to the South and North. That great cone is a huge signpost on the route northwards, covered by glistening white ice which the rays of the evening sun colour the most glorious crimson. And from its top a pillar of smoke wells up into the blue of the sky, which can be seen hundreds of miles out to sea in clear and calm weather.

It was a beautiful, but a savage, violent country, once long ago the dwelling place of thousands of Aleutians who had either perished under the harsh rule of the Russians or moved on to other parts to which the cruel, rapacious white man had not yet found his way.

We would have liked to have put in to the Pribylov Islands and enjoyed the sight of the millions of fur seals which come in the springtime from the Lord knows where in the Pacific to breed and mate on the rocky islands in the Bering Sea. But we did not dare. The *Duchess of Bedford* must have been particularly well known around the Pribylov Islands from the time when she was *Beatrice* and a busy poacher—and not for her virtue. What would we have done, what could we have done, if we had met an old acquaintance of *Beatrice's* who, with a cannon aimed at *Duchess of Bedford*, had presented an outstanding bill with a demand for immediate payment?

It would not have been much use protesting that *Duchess of Bedford* was a very respectable ship which carried the Royal Yacht Club's flag at the foretop and was on her way to unknown land in the Beaufort Sea. People are suspicious in that part of the world, and rightly so. Any ship can only too easily adopt some such disguise, and as we knew that both the American and the British, and perhaps even more so, the Russian—guard-ships had accounts outstanding with *Beatrice*, it was best to be careful and not risk coming to grief because of *Beatrice's* sins and depredations in the past. You should not tempt providence in such remote and relatively lawless parts as the Pribylov Islands.

Luckily there was room enough in the Bering Sea for us to be able to avoid going close to them, so we sailed in a wide arc round the dangerous spot and anchored on an open coast off the Mission and Trading Station, or perhaps more correctly Trading Station and Mission on St Lawrence Island. *Beatrice* would scarcely have been so far north on her lawless occasions, and there we felt safe.

Prominent in the centre of the trading post was a large two-storeyed house. To this we directed our steps and were received in the friendliest way by Dr Campbell, missionary teacher, administrator and doctor of a sort for the Eskimoes, though anywhere else his doctoring would have been called quackery. He also owned the one shop and all the goods in the large warehouses which stood close beside it. He was a trader before anything else, and had a share in every one of the Eskimoes' many whaling boats. He was everything there on the island, and the only white man among three or four hundred Eskimoes.

There was plenty for Dr Campbell to do, and he did a lot.

On Sundays he preached in the trading post's tiny little church, and every weekday he was school-teacher for an hour or two, but otherwise he was in the shop which was filled with lovely but most expensive goods. And as this was the only shop on the island, the Eskimoes had to buy everything they needed from the missionary. 'You must understand,' he said when I expressed a little surprise at the high prices, 'the trading profits don't go into my pocket, naturally not; they are used to maintain the mission and to pay the missionary's salary. You have to have something in return for spending years of your life in this lonely place—and among these people who haven't the least understanding of anything.'

Yes, we had already realized that apparently it was quite a lucrative business being trader, whaler and missionary in one and the same person—the many tons of whalebone in the warehouses, the great bundles of fine fox skins and the almost endless rows of barrels filled with whale-oil made that plain enough.

Dr Campbell was also a joiner, a house-builder. He had learned the trade out in the great world before he took to missionary work. His skill as a carpenter went hand in hand with his enterprise as a business man: for he was building one big house after another for the Eskimoes who bought the materials in Dr Cambel's shop and paid builder Campbell nice fat sums for his labours.

The Eskimoes proudly showed us their houses, which had three or four rooms, kitchen and stove and all the rest of it that a house ought to have. That, however, was about the only joy they had of their houses, for they were cold and uncomfortable, not because they lacked furniture, there was plenty of that and all bought in Campbell's shop, but naughty boys had used the windows as a target for their stones, perhaps even shot at them with rifles and almost all of them were broken.

It blows pretty hard in the Bering Sea and they say that you can count the number of days in the year when there is a calm on the fingers of one hand; and every gust of wind found its way through the broken windows, every storm, and there were many of those, went howling and whistling through the rooms where damp ran during the rainy summers and snow lay in drifts in the winter. The walls streamed and water gathered in great pools on the floors; fungi and rot flourished and thrived in those poor Eskimoes' lovely houses.

I have seldom been in such uncomfortable rooms as those in the wooden houses of Campbell's manufacture; and, when I had done my duty to the proud house-owner and unblushingly praised his treasure, it was a joy to get into the warmth and comfort of the hut in which the owner and his family actually lived, and which was built of local materials: driftwood, turf and big stones with every crevice stopped with moss and the whole covered with big walrus hides, a cosy weather-proof dwelling which the rigorous conditions had taught the Eskimoes' ancestors to build in the olden days.

All the same, a new motif had been introduced into the age-old structure of the huts: a little window inserted so as to face the lovely house—so that its owner could at least sit in the warmth and comfort and look out at the adjacent monstrosity which Campbell had built and the Eskimo paid for with tons of precious baleen.

They were enterprising people, those missionaries on the coast of Alaska, and even though as a rule they received no return for their missionary work, most of them became men of substance in a short time, since all their smaller or bigger side-lines brought them smaller or larger profits, and the shops—and especially the shares they all had in the whaling boats—brought them a big yearly income.

All the whites on the Alaskan coast in those days were only there to earn the greatest possible amount in the easiest possible manner. So why not the missionaries, too? To me it was distasteful to mix religion and business in that way; it inevitably had a rather depressing effect on those to whom money did not mean perhaps quite as much as it did to others. In the interests of truth let me say here that later we met missionaries who took their duties very seriously and who gave full value, but we also met those, who unfortunately were in the majority, with whom we were not proud to own kinship.

We bought dogs on St Lawrence Island, fine animals and not so very dear. Trader Campbell helped us and the Missionary Campbell demanded a sort of tithe of the barter goods with which we paid—for his missionary work, as he explained, was so expensive to maintain and 'we get no support worth mentioning from the States.'

We had gradually come to realize all that, so we gave the missionary what he demanded for his assistance—for the good of the cause!

We had intended to put into Nome on our way north, but we had now become rather afraid to do so, since just the winter before rich strikes had been made on the coast and in the mountains behind that little gold-mining town which till then had lain in complete obscurity. We had of course heard a good deal about the finds before we left Victoria, and from every ship we met as we sailed north it was like the refrain of a siren's song: 'There's gold in Nome, gold in Nome!' And big passenger steamers, so old and decrepit that several of them must have been on their very last voyages, slipped across the waters of the Bering Sea heading for Nome, crammed with gold-hungry men and women all certain that they would be able to appease their hunger if they could just get to Nome.

Now and then, too, we overheard our own crew talking covertly about gold in Nome, and there would be a guilty silence when they discovered that Leffingwell or I was listening. They were certainly contemplating something or other. The mate was already ill, very ill, so at least he said; and he asked us most urgently to be put ashore in Nome so that he could get better medical attention than what he felt our doctor could give him. Every time we saw him, he winced most horribly, for the poor man had pains in every joint—at least when we were near.

I was very afraid that our small crew would fall easy prey to the temptations to which Nome would expose them, and there was really nothing surprising in that. In Nome perhaps they would be able to earn a wage a hundred times as great as we could offer them—and then with us the reward was most uncertain, since it depended on our getting back with the *Duchess* intact. She was already leaking badly, and it was probable that the leak would grow even worse when we began struggling with the ice in earnest. *Duchess of Bedford* was no longer much of a security for a year or two's wages.

Thus it would really have been no wonder if our men had wanted to get to Nome to be among the first arrivals and have the chance to earn giant fortunes—nor if they were intending to desert if we got anywhere near that alluring town.

The most sensible thing was thus to make a large detour round Nome, as we had done with the Pribylov Islands, and when the news that this was what we intended got to the crew, black looks and mutterings fully confirmed our suspicions that it was Nome and not the Beaufort Sea which had been their objective. Passages from America to the gold country were difficult to get in those days, and also more expensive than a sailor could afford.

That too must have been the reason for the crew's magnanimous attitude over the size of their wages and why they had agreed with indulgent smiles to accept the ship as somewhat doubtful security for one or two years' pay. We might have spared our admiration for those fine young men whom we thought ready to renounce the enticements of Mammon for the unknown land in the north.

The wind was against us, and for days and weeks we had to tack up the Bering Sea towards the narrow Bering Strait where from the outermost point of Alaska you can see the cliffs on the most easterly point of Siberia looming above two small islands which lie right in the middle of the Strait only a mile or less from each other: the Diomedes Islands, Great and Little, the former Russian, the latter American.

It blew pretty hard out in the Strait, and there was a strong southerly current. We had to sail hard in order to beat into the Arctic Ocean, and often it seemed a hopeless labour trying to force the *Duchess* along against wind, seas and current without an auxiliary motor.

Slowly, infinitely slowly we made our way northwards, and each time we lay close-hauled heading for the Alaskan coast the light of hope lit in the eyes of the crew: perhaps now we were making for Nome after all. And whenever we lay on the other tack heading for the dark cliffs of Siberia, I kept a look-out across the swift waters of the Bering Straits for the torpedo boat which the Tsar might have sent to deny us access to the Arctic Ocean and the unknown land in the North—for we felt we might easily expect to see one after the fuss *Journal de St Petersbourg* had made a few months before.

But neither I nor any of the crew—it sounds so grand to be always talking about 'the crew,' but there were only four of them— saw what we were watching for. We saw neither the smoke of Nome, nor that of a Russian gunboat come to bar our way through the Straits.

We had to put in somewhere though, for we needed water and a few provisions before sailing farther into the great ocean, and so we steered into what we thought would be a safe place, one where desertion could not have had many attractions, the wonderful natural harbour of Port Clarence, on the Alaskan Coast, some seventy miles from Nome.

The first white man to come aboard was Mr Bewin, a missionary of the right kind, who without thought of worldly profit gathered the Eskimoes round him, both grown-ups and little ones, especially the latter.

He was a fine person that Bewin. He and his wife, who were both Norwegians, had been at Port Clarence for a good many years. Round them swarmed a flock of some fifty orphan children who lived with them, and though he gave them some instruction in religion and Christian ways, he paid most attention to teaching the boys the use of tools of all kinds. Mrs Bewin would have had enough to do with her huge household, yet she also taught the girls, cleanliness in the first place, but also all the things a woman must know how to do if she is to be a good housewife in an Eskimo home—which several of her pupils were already, living in big wooden houses, as clean and neat as Mrs Bewin's own.

They worked by way of example those two missionaries, who had left their home in the most northerly part of Norway in order to show the Eskimoes at Port Clarence the way to a better life than the only one they had been able to know before. They lived their own lives strictly in accordance with what they preached to the Eskimoes. Everyone, their friends and also their enemies, admitted that. And they had their enemies, for some of the Whites in Port Clarence still had the old-fashioned idea that the Eskimoes were only half-human and could and should be exploited to one's own advantage. And that they had been doing with a vengeance until the Bewins came.

When we anchored in Port Clarence, there was a white barque in the roads, a lovely ship, gleaming with cleanliness and polished brass. This was the revenue cutter *Thetis*, a famous craft which had done wonders on the relatively lawless coast of Alaska as its one and only upholder of law and justice. Her commander was Captain O. C. Hamlet, a splendid man who later gave us many a helping hand. Now he sent a boat across to invite us aboard. With the boat came a young lieutenant who gave us a letter from Captain Hamlet saying: 'While you are over with us, the lieutenant will stay aboard *Duchess of Bedford* to keep an eye on your crew. Nome

47

is comparatively near and that is a danger for any but the most steadfast.'

Thus we were able to leave our ship safely and spend the evening in the revenue cutter, where we were given good advice and promised every possible assistance if we got in a fix: 'Keep a sharp eye on your crew, my friend,' said the old and experienced Captain, 'they will desert if you give them the slightest chance. And if you need strong arms to help you, just hoist a flag at the foretop and we'll come at once.'

I laughed and said: 'Nome is over seventy miles away across trackless tundra, that surely should cure even the worst gold fever.' But Hamlet just shrugged his shoulders: 'You'll see,' he said. 'But take my advice. I know sailors and men on this coast, and I know how violent gold-fever can be.'

He was right. We had to call for help the very next morning. Our four had decamped at daybreak. They had taken the dinghy and rowed across to Teller, a tiny hole with some hard-boiled gold-diggers as its only inhabitants.

We tried amicable persuasion but all our arguments just bounced off the armour with which the advice of the locals and the nearness of gold had furnished them. Then we tried sterner talk, but they were most unwilling to go back aboard the little *Duchess of Bedford*; they laughed at our warnings to remember what desertion meant for them and for us, and they told us shamelessly that they had only signed on in the wretched boat in order to get to Alaska for nothing. Now at least they had got there and there they intended to remain, however much we protested. And they and their grinning friends became so foul-mouthed and threatening that we had to withdraw and row back to our empty ship without accomplishing anything.

But hoist the flag to the foretop we could and did, a fluttering cry for help, and shortly afterwards a boat came across from *Thetis* with ten stalwart men in her: 'Come along, and we'll see about this!'

We rowed to the shore where we had been so ignominiously

sent packing a short while before—but now the boot was on the
other foot: our deserters' friends were sour enough when shortly
afterwards we rowed back and took the four aboard our lovely
Duchess of Bedford of which they had spoken so contemptuously just
an hour before.

Our position, however, was pretty precarious, and if we were
ever going to get the ship away from Port Clarence we had to leave
straight away. The men from *Thetis* helped us get the anchor up,
while Hamlet told me what best to do: 'Run up to Point Hope and
drop anchor off Jabbertown, we'll meet again there in a few days'
time. It's still too early to go into the ice, and you'll have plenty
of time to get there. It is said to be very heavy this year.'

Our good relations with the crew had been destroyed. The men
had openly shown their hand: Nome was where they were making
for; they were not thinking of spending one or two winters on the
harsh coast of North Alaska, and certainly not on the unknown
land out there in the wilderness of ice.

At least we knew that now, and we who lived aft had many
grave talks about the future: what should we do, what *could* we
do? To go into the ice with a reluctant crew, men who were only
kept aboard by compulsion, could only bring the expedition to
grief.

49

CHAPTER V

NORTHWARDS ALONG THE ALASKAN
COAST

*Point Hope—A new crew—Desperate ice conditions—Bold sailing gives
a good result—America's most northerly point—Meeting with Gjøa and
Amundsen—Lawlessness in Alaska—Whalers in a fix—Afflictions of the
Eskimoes—Winter harbour*

WE reached Jabbertown and anchored a good way off shore, for
though it was over three hundred miles overland to Nome and
about as far by boat, you could never tell what people might not
attempt when in the delirium of violent gold fever.

Some days later the white revenue cutter came in and anchored
near us. Captain Hamlet came aboard and held a court at which
the four were tried for attempted desertion and sentenced to be put
ashore immediately, a pretty hard punishment. He had comfort
too for me who saw my crew being whisked away before my eyes:
'I have four good men aboard *Thetis* who will gladly sail with you,'
said he.

Good for you, Hamlet, now we could breathe again. Then after
one of the four we were going to maroon, a Norwegian and a
brilliant seaman, Storker Storkersen, had forsworn the error of
his ways and been promoted to mate, we got three men from
Thetis and made ready to set the gold-hungry three ashore on a
coast which must be one of the most desolate in the world.

The three looked in horror at the desolate coast on which there
lived some four hundred Eskimoes and one splendid white man,
Dr Driggs, a missionary, a man who would stand no nonsense,
and who had recently kicked out some so-called missionaries who
had come to Point Hope in order to be near the place where
earthly Mammon was to be had for the mere labour of picking it up.

The three culprits promised most solemnly they would behave
in the future, a promise which of course we did not dare rely on,

and with the friendly assistance of the grinning, but heavy-handed lads from *Thetis* we got them into a boat and on to the shore, where they sat on their kit-bags and gazed dejectedly towards the south, where lay Nome and the goal of their longings, the land of gold. Now they could do what they liked: tramp across the marshy tundra to Nome or find a chance ship which might be willing to take them so far. Or else they could stay at Point Hope till a whaling boat came in on its way south to San Francisco, and in the meantime live with the Eskimoes, eating their food of which they had an abundance, though it would hardly be as much to their taste as what they were accustomed to on board the *Duchess*.

The three we marooned could come to no harm there; Dr Driggs and the Eskimoes' usual helpfulness were guarantees of that, but the summer would be no more pleasant for them than they deserved—which wasn't much.

Thetis was also intending to go north to Point Barrow where Captain Hamlet had to try a number of whalers who had been frozen in by Herschel Island the previous year, where their behaviour to the Eskimoes had been so outrageous that reports of it had even reached more law-abiding parts.

Several other ships came up from the south and were halted by the ice at Jabbertown, where gradually quite a little fleet of steam-driven ships assembled, and then of course there was our little *Duchess of Bedford* which only had her sails to rely on.

Time passed slowly, though we led a pleasant comfortable life and enjoyed the hospitality of all the other ships. But the enforced wait pleased no one. In the polar regions the summer is brief and much has to be accomplished, much money made by the whalers, before the new ice binds the floes together and makes sailing impossible. No one dare stay in the ice later than the end of August, unless, like us, he is prepared to winter there.

We all only wanted to get away, but reports of conditions up north were all agreed: there was still far too much ice. *Thetis* set out to try it on behalf of the others and we hoped for good news; but Captain Hamlet had to turn back after being away only a few hours and had no comfort for us on his return: even *Thetis* with her powerful engines had not been able to get beyond Cape Lisburne, and the ice was heavy as far as could be seen to the north and west.

So we had to wait and wait while the summer passed and with it our hopes of a swift and easy sail along the coast. Yet we still had a long way to sail before we could let our anchor go in some part which would be convenient for reaching our journey's end.

It was intolerable having to wait. We wanted, no, we *had* to get away, if we were even to be able to hope to achieve anything in that year to which we had looked forward with such great expectations.

I looked at the chart just to have something to do and mentally traced the route we should have to sail. And then it suddenly struck me that there probably must be a narrow channel of open water between the shallow coast and the grounded ice, a channel with so little water that bigger ships had to keep away, though our little *Duchess of Bedford* would be able to sail where others would run aground.

Should we risk it? I knew that it would be a rash thing to do—but it was always better than that eternal waiting.

We naturally discussed our idea with those who knew the coast and the ice, and they all advised us most definitely not to attempt it: it would never work, they said. But all the same—we were stubborn and it was as tempting to get moving again as to try and accomplish what others said we couldn't do. We held a ship's council: 'The situation is such and such—the summer is passing—we've a long way to sail before winter stops all further progress—the pack-ice probably grounds in three fathoms of water—we only draw one and a half. What do you say, lads, shall we risk it?'

We looked at the charts, such as they were in those primitive days, certainly not too good. It looked as though there would be a chance; it might just come off. We were young, tired of waiting and, no doubt, a bit rash. Long reflection was not for us, would not get us nearer our goal, we might just as well make the attempt as remain there at anchor off Jabbertown till we became old and grey.

The old hands who knew the Arctic Ocean shook their heads resignedly at the recklessness of youth as they saw us weigh anchor, dip our flag and round the most westerly point of America with a fair wind drawing.

It came off, but it was a hard tussle. The shore-water was there as we expected, and the pack-ice was also grounded as we expected. But unfortunately there were any number of sandbanks which the charts never mentioned, and then unfortunately we met head-winds. And that was an eventuality we had never taken into consideration. And a head-wind was the worst thing which could have happened to us, for that meant that if we were to make any progress northwards we had to tack in a very narrow channel where we had sandbanks or the shore to the east and the impenetrable pack-ice to the west.

It was a tough job, very tough. It was 'bout ship and 'bout again, to and fro with close-hauled sheets in that narrow shore-water: off-shore till we ran into an icefloe and went about; shoreward, till the lowered anchor took bottom and swung the ship up into the wind. Then quickly up with the anchor and fill the sails for the westward stretch out to the ice again.

Everyone aboard toiled inhumanly, hauling on the sheets and falls or heaving on the anchor. From the moment we began sailing till, exhausted, we had to cry a halt, or mist came and forced us to stay where we were, we were kept running to and fro between the slapping foresail and the mainsail sheets. No one thought of food, or rather, we thought of it, but no one had time to do anything about it; we kept a tin of biscuits on the hatch, and now and again we would snatch one or two on our everlasting career between bows and stern.

The seemingly easiest job was mine, for from the moment we first forged ahead in the early morning till one imperative reason or other caused us to stop, I directed manoeuvres from a lofty stance in the fore crosstrees, where I clung to a stay or guy-rope, swept by the icy wind, chilled to the marrow and with hands and feet numb with cold.

It was, however, essential to endure it up there, for from that height I could see the bottom and judge pretty well if there was enough water for us or whether we must go about and hold out towards the ice, watching for the long ice-spurs there: these were as hard as rock, and it wouldn't have done the hull much good if we had bumped into them too hard or too often. It couldn't be avoided altogether, and if we caught one badly, or if it had a sharp edge, splinters from the ship's teak bottom swirled up alongside. Once or twice when we struck especially hard, quite big bits of wood from keel or stem came up and bobbed in our wake astern.

If we missed stays, then she had to wear round and got too much speed up and banged into the ice so violently that I was almost shaken off my precarious perch. At such times the old ship sighed and groaned; the masts quivered as though they were about to go overboard; shouted orders from the mast-top and hoarse answers from the deck crossed each other in the air; the sails hammered and cracked like thunder; the water gurgled and boiled round us and made its way into the ship through the open seams. We had to pump ship as well at times; all could be confusion and imminent disaster one moment, and the next we would have sailed clear of the ice and be forging ahead through open water towards the shore. But we all had an unpleasant feeling that the ship was being flayed to pieces under our feet.

It was hard sailing, too hard, and Leffingwell who had joint command of the expedition with me, was quite right when, after an exceptionally hard collision, he called up to me querying whether I wasn't being irresponsible.

It was in a way irresponsible, but also inevitable, since we had deliberately elected to attempt the dangerous business of beating north between the ice and land. Well, not of beating, for we had forgotten to take the wind into consideration. By the time it turned against us, there was no going back, and we had to continue as we were, come what might.

So we struggled on, contending with ice, sandbanks, land and mist, and also with the damned headwind. But on the twelfth day after leaving Jabbertown we ran into a large clear expanse off Point Barrow and anchored opposite the trading post as the first ship of the year. We were tired, but pleased, and not a little proud of our feat. Two days later *Thetis* arrived with five or six steam-schooners in her train.

All things considered we hadn't so much to shout about, for to the east, on the other side of Point Barrow which was where we were making for and where we ought to have been three weeks before, the ice was still packed tight against the land. There was no water visible, and the overcast sky reflected only ice and ice again, as far as you could see.

Evening after evening reddish-golden colours of sunset welled out over a wilderness of ice in the west, and morning after morning the sun kindled a blazing bonfire over ice to the east. The nights were beginning to lengthen, the stars glittered like diamonds in the dark night sky, and a gleaming moon made its sedate way each night between east and west. The summer was almost over, and the frost was building bridges between the ice-floes; winter was threateningly near.

One fine morning when we had almost resigned ourselves to the idea that we were not going to be able to make our way farther east, hope was rekindled by the sight of a little sloop rounding Point Barrow from the east. She came and anchored alongside us. This was *Gjøa* with Roald Amundsen in command, having success-fully sailed the North-West Passage, the first ship ever to do so. We were thus able to be the first to congratulate Amundsen and his crew on their feat, and as it seemed logical that where one ship could sail one way another ship could also sail the other way, we decided to make the attempt.

We got up the anchor and set out full of hope. We soon discovered, however, that *Duchess of Bedford* drew two feet more than *Gjøa* which had been able to slip across sandbanks where the *Duchess* took ground. After a day and night's labour during which we ran aground several times and had some hard bumps into the ice, we had to abandon the attempt and brought our dispirited duck-

55

ling of a ship to rest alongside big *Thetis* where she could be sheltered from ice and weather.

There was not much encouragement for us anywhere, and however hard it might be, we had to resign ourselves to what, I suppose, is the worst fate which can overtake the young and enterprising, that of having to wait and wait without being able to do anything to shorten the time of waiting. There was nothing for it, but to wait patiently for open water, or slack ice— which *perhaps* would come, perhaps not, before the autumn storms drove us ashore or into the lagoon behind Point Barrow, where we would have a whole year to wait before the ice would break up.

It didn't turn out quite as bad as that, and one day we were rewarded for our enforced and more or less patient wait by seeing across the low land the masts of ten or so whalers laboriously working their way through the ice towards us. They at last were proof that the ice was now so open that we perhaps would soon be able to sail on east.

Great was our delight to see the whalers steam round the low sandy promontory of Point Barrow, but they can scarcely have shared it when they found that they had run right into the arms of the law in the shape of *Thetis*, whose duty it was to board each whaling steamer in search of evidence for or against the nasty rumours which had escaped from the frozen silent North and been carried thousands of miles across lawless Alaska till, somehow or other they had reached the ears of those who sat in the government offices in Washington—ugly rumours of the whalers' brutal and ruthless behaviour towards the defenceless Eskimoes, of robbery and plundering and abuse of numbers of women.

Captain Hamlet, who gave us such friendly smiles, had none for the whalers. Each time one of their ships emerged into the open water just west of Point Barrow, he forced her to anchor and sent officers on board to investigate conditions in her. The officers had orders that if they found women on board, they and the whaler's skipper were to be taken at once to *Thetis*.

Rumour had not exaggerated: the whalers were carrying num-

56

bers of women, many of them under age. One skipper, an old hunchback of a man, had five little girls on board to amuse himself with during the long dark winter, the eldest of whom was only thirteen.

He was immediately removed from his ship and kept under arrest in *Thetis*. Other skippers followed him, mates and chief engineers as well; there were plenty of lightning promotions in that whaling fleet. But the bitterness was very great. Until then people had been able to do pretty well just what they liked in those parts, and no one had interfered. If you got away with it, so much the better; if you didn't, but went under, well, it wasn't such a great disaster either. That had been the rule for both white men and Eskimoes.

But now all that was over, and the resentful whalers huddled together in *Thetis*, muttering bitterly against the representatives of law and decency and gazing contemptuously at the host of women and children Captain Hamlet had removed from their ships to the revenue cutter where they were safe under his paternal care—even though it was only too obvious that several of the women would have preferred to have spent their time with the angry skippers.

Hamlet told us about the lawlessness which had infected Alaska especially after the discovery of gold there had attracted a lot of human flotsam who did nothing to advance virtue or morals. That had to be changed, was going to be changed; America could not do otherwise. And now it had become Hamlet's job to clean up the whaling fleet. No wonder that the crews were furious at that uncalled-for interference with their licentious doings.

It was not only the whalers Hamlet was out for, but also the many other white men whom adversity had compelled to leave civilization and who had found a refuge on the coast in the lawless North. Many of those men were not much good whatever their occupation, and several were worse than the whalers—and that's saying a lot.

Hamlet told us of one missionary who for several years had lived a little farther down the coast, not far from Point Hope. One of his many lucrative sidelines was that of providing the whaling fleet with women to take with them into the ice—whom he then welcomed back the following year when they returned with the provisions and other things the whalers had given them for their services.

One year the ships returned after an unusually long stay in the ice, with their provisions and supplies all used up. As the whalers had none of the usual means of payment, the Eskimoes, both the men and the women, had to take in part payment of their wages a number of great barrels of treacle—the only thing of which the ships still had a surplus.

So, the whalers sailed on southwards, leaving the Eskimoes looking somewhat askance at all this treacle they had got.

It was delicious when eaten in moderation—but it wasn't so good in large quantities. What were they to do with their boundless wealth of treacle? Even the dogs soon got sick of it and kept away from the great barrels.

But the missionary knew what to do. He invited the entire population, which was considerable, to a feast at which he treated them to spirits and other delicacies. The next morning the thirsty Eskimoes came to him asking to be allowed to buy a little alcohol to moisten their dry gums. The missionary wasn't very interested in selling it, but didn't they have lots of treacle? You could turn that into alcohol; in fact what they had drunk the day before had been made from the small quantity the missionary had received as his share.

How was it done? The Eskimoes were now most interested, thinking of all the barrels of treacle they had left.

So, for a considerable amount of valuable furs and fine baleen the missionary taught the Eskimoes the art of distilling spirits from the sweet sticky treacle.

That winter was a bad one for the Eskimo population there. They drank till they dropped—and the cold did the rest. They drank and drew their knives on friends and enemies, and death and mutilation rode on whistling rifle bullets about the settlement, striking indiscriminately. Others drank to give themselves warmth and courage before they went out hunting, and often fell easy prey to the cold, a blizzard or a stalking bear, or else they capsized their kayaks and drowned in the icy water. When the sun returned at the end of that evil winter over half the population of that settlement had died as a direct consequence of their dearly-bought knowledge of how to transform treacle into intoxicating fusel. Others were on the verge of starvation, for none had been able to catch sufficient to maintain life properly. But the missionary didn't see all the misery he had caused, for by then he had gone south, well satisfied with what he had made out of the lawless North.

It was that sort of thing Captain Hamlet was to stop and punish. But the whalers and the whites of the coast fumed: what did it concern him, that uniformed flunkey of a so-and-so government office in Washington?

At the end of August *Belvedere*, a whaler, came in from the east and anchored like all the others near *Thetis*. The hour of reckoning had struck for her too. Her skipper had sinned like all the others in the whaling fleet, but perhaps not as badly as most, and Hamlet told him that as he was relatively guiltless, if he would help the *Duchess* eastward through the worst of the ice, Hamlet would temper justice with mercy and let him off.

The skipper agreed, and very glad he was to do so; so we said goodbye to our friend Hamlet and the fine crew of *Thetis*, and headed eastward in the wake of the steam-driven whaler and so came unscathed through the seven or eight mile broad barrier of sandbanks, reefs and grounded ice, which had held us up so long. After that we could look after ourselves, for a while at least, for autumn had come, the heavens were resplendent, there was crisp frost, and new ice covered the sea with shining armour which had tinkled as it was broken by the whaler's iron-clad stem.

It was high time we found suitable winter quarters, and that as soon as possible. Our reason told us that, and so did the experienced whaler skipper before we took leave of each other. 'Don't be stubborn and try to get further east this year,' he said, 'It's altogether too late, especially with a sailing vessel. You'd much better get a snug winter harbour at Point Barrow, and wait till next year for your sledge journey. Life is long for people as young as you. Don't risk too much just for the sake of ambition. The ice has been too stout an opponent for you this year; maybe it will be more obliging next summer.'

It was all very well for him to talk, that well-intentioned whaling skipper, but we had only one year's provisions on board—and no money to buy more. And there to the north-east lay the land, the unknown land, we were out to discover.

It was hard to give up now. In fact we had gone too far to be able to do that, so we thanked him for his well-meant and no doubt quite correct advice, ran up under *Belvedere's* stern, dipped our flag and after that our ways parted: *Belvedere* hastened west-wards to Point Barrow, and we set course eastwards in the full knowledge that we must endure a hard fight with ice and currents and all sorts of difficulties, not least of which was the fact that the *Duchess* was leaking like a sieve.

We were alone in the Beaufort Sea and saw the myriads of the migrant birds winging their way across the seemingly unbroken mass of the pack-ice—from the land in the north-east to the sunny smiling south

CHAPTER VI

JOYS AND SORROWS OF THE
POLAR WINTER

The Eskimo Sachawachiak—Life with the Eskimoes—Hunting and fishing—Rabies—We start sledging across the pack-ice—Sachawachiak reports us as having perished

WINTER came with storms and swirling driving snow, with sparkling clear air, flickering Northern Lights, blazing stars and a moon so brilliant that it seemed to have stolen the sun's radiance. And though the winter was long, it was also good, for the gods so arranged it that our enforced winter quarters were close to Flaxman Island where some Eskimoes lived. They were a joy and an object lesson to us, and we of some advantage to them, for they shared in the relative luxury of our provisions.

Those Eskimoes on Flaxman Island became our friends. They had gone out into the wilds there some years before, leaving Point Barrow with its many Eskimoes and the few white men who ruled them with a hard hand, harder than our freeborn Eskimo friends could stomach. Sachawachiak and his splendid wife Douglamana, in particular, had suffered from the heavy-handed rule of the white man, and they no longer wanted to be where the white man was. So they had moved out into the wilderness and on Flaxman Island had built themselves a hut of driftwood and turf, covered with thick walrus hide, made it snug and good and stout, the right sort of hut to stand up to the rigorous arctic weather. There Sachawachiak had lived for a number of years, getting enough for his family to live on by hunting on sea or land, as his ancestors had done for many generations before the white man came to their country with new ways which were not to the Eskimoes' advantage.

We had heard Sachawachiak spoken of in Point Barrow as a great man among the Eskimoes, the best hunter and trapper on the coast, a great catcher of whales. But that he had been chucked out by the whites, and now set his fox-traps far to the east and west along the coast and inland right up to the mountains whose massive sharp silhouettes you could see rising blue with distance in the south, high above the tundra which abounded in game and where caribou roamed in huge herds.

There was game enough there for an active man. Sachawachiak was his own master there and respected by his fellow tribesmen. There he could practise on land and ice the dangerous craft of the hunter which he had inherited from his ancestors and which he would hand on to the next generation. There Sachawachiak felt free of his white tormentors who had taken everything from the Eskimoes at Point Barrow: their women and their ancestral hunting grounds on land—even the whales in the sea off the coast, which in the olden days the Eskimoes had hunted and killed with their few poor weapons, had now become the white man's—though it was still the natives who had to catch them, not for their own benefit, but to make money for their masters.

On Flaxman Island Sachawachiak had hitherto been free of the white horde, who took and took without giving anything but disease and misery in return—and then we had arrived at that island, where some other Eskimoes as well as Sachawachiak had sought solitude and freedom from the white man.

Sachawachiak and Douglamana could certainly not have welcomed our arrival, but we never noticed the fact. We were conceited and simple enough to believe that the Eskimoes would be highly delighted to have us as neighbours during the harsh winter which was at hand. They helped us in every way they could, with work, advice and the best food they had, bringing us large pieces of juicy caribou meat, glistening salmon and also ptarmigan in such numbers that we grew tired of them.

We in our turn had a few things the Eskimos liked and were just as lavish with them as the Eskimoes with their presents. We gave and the Eskimoes gave, and that was as it should have been. Their resentment of our arrival at their peaceful island gradually dissipated, and it was only much later that we realized that in the beginning we had been regarded as disturbers of their peace. We became real friends, we respected each other and helped each other as well as we could.

It proved a good winter for us all, and our relations with the Eskimoes remained the best possible. We spent many instructive hours in their snug huts; we went sledging together into parts where white men had not yet been and where we met the inland Eskimoes who dwelt among the mountains and only seldom came to the coast.

There were magnificent autumn trips along the banks of the great rivers which had tall bushes that could break the force of the storm as it swept across the land, driving the snow ahead of it like an army of attacking ghosts, or would crackle and glow in the little stove in our tent and warm us, as when we were weather-bound on Kookerakook.

There were lots of salmon in the river, big fat ones, and we could sit snugly on a box in our tent and fish or harpoon the magnificent things through a hole in the ice. That provided a good supply of winter provisions, yet better still were the big herds of caribou which roamed the frozen, windswept tundra, seeking shelter where there was shelter to be found. But those places were also known to the Eskimoes, and there we would lie in wait.

When the shots rang out the frightened beasts would rush about confusedly, trying to escape. We shot many, but we could use many, for the winter was long and cold. It was hard work haul-ing the huge loads of meat and hides back to our camp, where fires flamed in the dark night and the women were kept busy, boiling and roasting the enormous quantities of juicy meat that tired hungry hunters can put away after a long day, during which they have covered a lot of country.

The winter came with howling storms and blinding snow; but it also passed, as winters do, however long and dark they may be; that of 1906–07 was no different and ended without having proved in any way too rigorous for us in the comfort of our cosy ship. Our greatest events were the visits of the Eskimoes to us and ours to them, for the daylight was too short for us to be able to go far from the ship, so we stayed comfortably on board, attending to our own affairs and getting ready for our dash across the ice.

If the weather was reasonable we went hunting with the Eskimoes, and I was often with Sachawachiak out by the open water where the ice-pack, impelled by wind and current, crashed against the fixed land-ice with a tremendous din and great splashings when ice-blocks weighing scores of tons toppled into the sea from the top of the huge pressure ridges which piled up where the ice met.

Even in the depths of winter, when out by the channel of open water, we might have the luck to get a shot at a seal or walrus, and it was no rarity for a solitary bear to come wandering across the pack-ice, its small head lifted up towards the clouds until the scent of us tickled its nostrils and it started to hunt us.

As a rule we disposed of the bear without much fuss, but sometimes one would come stalking up on us without our noticing it until it was quite close. That could be dangerous, but we always had our rifles at hand; shots would ring out, the bear would give an ugly hiss and a roar and try to escape from what was stronger than it was, which it seldom succeeded in doing. Rifles were too much for it. And when the bear was dead, skinned and quartered, pots would be bubbling in the little huts along the shore, while in the galley of *Duchess of Bedford* we grilled bear-steaks enough to feed an army.

Sachawachiak was a good hunting companion, always ready to take the heavier burden, the more dangerous position, and he loved telling how, as a child and half in play, he had learnt the art of hunting the animals of the polar seas before the advent of the white man and his rifle. Many a time I have been amazed by the accuracy with which he could throw his harpoon when the round head of a seal had broken surface even quite a distance from the edge of the ice.

One day we were out as usual, Sachawachiak and I. The weather was good and it was fairly light. As we sat on an ice-hillock scanning the ice for seal or bear, Sachawachiak told me how in the old days—before guns—the Eskimoes used to kill bears with a harpoon, and how he had learned to do that when he was young.

And then a bear came.

Sachawachiak laid his hand on my arm and whispered that though it was a longish time since he had killed a bear with a harpoon, he was still not too old to do so again; and with urgent instructions to me not to intervene however great the danger might seem to be, he gave me his rifle to look after, picked up the harpoon and walked towards the bear with slow steps.

Soon the bear discovered the man, but as it also wanted to observe the rules of the game, its approach was most cautious: it hid behind hillocks of ice, made long detours and took plenty of time about everything.

In the end the two hunters, man and bear, had to leave their cover and so found themselves face to face on a smooth floe. The hunt ought to have been all but over, yet to my amazement Sachawachiak let out a roar, turned and ran off across the ice as fast as he could away from the great brute of a bear, which stood there hissing at him and growling angrily.

This presumably was what the bear had been waiting for; now it had its prey where it wanted, in full flight with terror at his heels, so the bear set off after Sachawachiak in long bounds, and gained on him so quickly that I became anxious; had Sachawachiak suddenly grown afraid and run for his life?

My rifle was loaded, the hammer cocked, and I kept the sights trained on the galloping bear ready to intervene with a killing shot. But my promise not to interfere, however wrong the hunt might seem to have gone for Sachawachiak, kept me from actually firing at the bear, which was now right at the Eskimo's heels.

Sachawachiak was fast, but the bear faster still, almost upon him—then the Eskimo jumped to the right and, turning like lightning, faced the bear, his body bent forward, legs straddled and harpoon raised. The bear could not change direction so swiftly and suddenly as the man; its great heavy body went slithering round as it turned, and the moment for which Sachawachiak had been waiting and which he had called forth by his run and leap to the side, had arrived: expertly he thrust the harpoon into the bear, which literally impaled itself, and without even a gasp the great powerful animal dropped with its heart pierced, and Sachawachiak waved to me grinning, and called out: 'That's how my father taught me to kill bears, and that's how my sons will also be able to kill them. Rifles are good enough for women— and for you white men!'

It was a fantastically brave way of hunting. If the harpoon had touched a bone, the man would have been knocked down by the collision with the bear and killed: it was man's courage and hunting skill set against the blind strength of the wild animal. It was a magnificent spectacle.

Scarcely a day passed all that long winter without our being with Sachawachiak and Douglamana, either on board the *Duchess*, or—what we preferred—in their warm hut where their two little boys tumbled about as free and uninhibited as the young of wild animals on the tundra or ice.

We listened with interest to the tales the old Eskimoes had to tell, often most instructive and strange to us, especially those of the land out there in the north which Sachawachiak himself had glimpsed on several occasions. His father had even known the great Eskimo traveller who had made the lone journey across the ice to the land beyond the horizon where the beautiful fat women dwelt. That was edifying talk for us to hear, but whenever we got on to the subject and told Sachawachiak that we intended going out there, he would look worried and shake his head: 'Give up the project, my friends; many Eskimoes have gone across the ice to the land out there, but they have never come back. Only the one, that man from Point Barrow. And perhaps he was not telling the truth about the fat women there.'

We tried to explain to Sachawachiak that it was the land, not the fat women, which interested us, but he could not understand that. The women—yes, at a pinch, though he personally felt that Douglamana was probably just as good as the ones out there in that wilderness of ice. But the land? No, that he found incomprehensible, there was more than enough land right where we were. What did we want more for? What would we do with the land?

'Let the land be,' he advised us with a worried look in his handsome brown eyes—'don't go out on to the pack-ice. You'll never come back. Either the women will keep you there, or you will die in the pack-ice. You had much better stay here where it is so good to be.'

So it was. We enjoyed that winter on Flaxman Island where we lived in close association with the Eskimoes who came to us with their joys, both great and small, but said nothing of their sorrows and cares, though they had those as well now and again. If we asked the Eskimoes for help, it was as a rule given most willingly, and they knew how to deal with almost every situation which could arise in their country.

There was, unfortunately, one thing with which they could not deal, and that was rabies. Shortly after we anchored at Flaxman Island some of our dogs began showing symptoms which could only be attributed to that dreadful scourge. The Eskimoes' dogs were also affected, but when we asked them about means of combating the disease, they just shrugged their shoulders and told us with stoical calm that it was a thing which came to the coast off and on, that it could be pretty bad, many dogs would die, and perhaps the Eskimoes would have to get along for a year or two without dogs. But what was the use of complaining? The epidemic would stop some time, and gradually they would get dogs again.

They, of course, could take the dread disease with equanimity, for they could always stay at home and had no need to gad about the country behind a dog team; but we had only come so far in order that we could—and would—go farther still by dog team. We had a pack of some fifty animals, and that number was essential if we were to have any prospect of success when we set out on our sledge journey towards the unknown land.

Even before winter had set in in earnest we had been forced to shoot several of our precious animals in the hope of limiting the outbreak. But it seemed to do no good, fresh cases kept occurring, and the sick animals rushed howling to and fro between the ship and the land, biting and snapping indiscriminately and spreading the sickness with every bite.

It happened, too, and not so seldom either, that we received a bite from an infected dog which came rushing at us with froth round its mouth. We were frightened of those bites and always carried a weapon so that we could stop an attack with a mortal blow. Even so, the dogs often bit us before we could use our short cudgel loaded with lead at the heavy end. Dr Howe, our doctor, was especially worried, as he well might be, and told us horrible tales about the consequences of being bitten by mad dogs. He insisted that each should always carry a caustic stick and summon one of the others at once if he was bitten, so that the other could cauterize the wound with the painful stick. Most of us didn't have the nerve to burn our own wounds as deep as was necessary to neutralize the poison, which the bite might have implanted in us.

The Eskimoes, of course, were right. The disease spread; there was no way of combating it, so why worry about what we couldn't change? They didn't shoot their infected dogs, which as a rule died in the course of a few days. And if they themselves received a bite from an infected dog they did not worry in the least about it. Ignorance is often beneficial to one's peace of mind.

The poor *Duchess* herself was not in too good a shape and showed unmistakable signs of the defects and dilapidation of old age, precipitated to some extent, perhaps considerably, by the rough treatment she had had to endure from the ice and the sand-banks along the Alaskan shore.

Now she was frozen in the ice, a defenceless prey to its rough whims and those of the winter. The hull creaked and groaned, and sometimes there would be a report like a gun as some bit of timber somewhere was split by the iron grip of the frost. It sounded most weird and uncanny, especially when, as she did at times, the

68

whole ship moaned like a person in distress. Thick ice formed round the outside, and that too gave vent to sighs and laments as the bitter cold split it. If one of these frost-cracks struck the ship she would sometimes shift slightly in her dry dock of ice and lean exhaustedly against the thick ice, as though seeking support and rest.

Winter went its course. The solstice came and went, and then a faint glow began to appear in the southern sky about midday and for a short while withdrew the tall straggling mountains far inland out of the darkness and gave depth to the snow-covered landscape. It was lovely to behold and a promising sight, for it meant that, where at noon a glow now tinged the snow and ice with the faintest pink, there before so very long the sun would rise in all its golden might to announce the spring and the coming of summer, to rouse the creatures of the tundra and ice from their torpor, and bring from the south the myriads of migrant birds, which during the short but hectic summer made the north a place of life like few others in the world.

And when the sun had at length returned after several months' hibernation, when the storms had finally exhausted themselves after a short final bout of raging and howling about the tundra as though to greet the sun's arrival, when our winter-weary bodies imagined they could feel the emanation of a slight mildness from the reddish-golden disc of the sun, that was when we had to be ready for our great sledge journey across the Beaufort Sea to— yes, to what? Land, we hoped, and our Eskimo friends were sure that we would find land if we managed to get out so far on to the ice. But they were equally certain that we would never return to them: the wilderness of ice to the north, the living, ever-changing pack-ice never surrendered those who had given themselves into its power.

Sachawachiak, in particular, was worried. That intelligent Eskimo, who had so much experience of the ice, and of life in the Arctic, regarded our intended sledge journey across the pack-ice as a desperate and reckless act. And yet—when the day came and our sledges stood laden alongside our somewhat battered *Duchess of Bedford*, he appeared with two of his remaining four dogs and a light sledge: 'The dogs are for you,' he said. 'You have been good to us and are not like other white men I have known. You have more need of the dogs than I. On the sledge I have a few things I shall need so that I can get myself back to land—when I decide not to go further with you.'

Was he intending to go out on to the pack-ice? Yes, he was, but only for a short distance. For though we were clever and knew much more than he, he knew the ice better than we. He was going to help us over the first difficult stretch, which was where all winter masses of drifting ice had been continually pounding at the land-ice, splintering it in lumps and pieces and being itself shattered in the collision, and had thereby formed a hell of broken, splintered and compressed ice, that was never at rest, a live quivering mass, which in bad weather with a storm blowing on land could be piled up with a great din and commotion in ramparts thirty to fifty feet high at the point where land and pack-ice met.

We knew that ice. Many times during the winter we had sat out there by the outer fringe of the land-ice, watching and listening to the Titans playing their demoniac games with hundreds, perhaps thousands of tons of ice. And we had dreaded the thought of that ice, the water between the ice-floes and that which was worst of all, what was neither ice nor water, but porridge-ice, which might bear or might not, just as the case might be; and we had wondered how we were ever going to get across that hell and reach the ice which was as ice ought to be.

Here now was Sachawachiak voluntarily offering to help us across that dreadful first stretch which we had to cross, if we were to get anywhere. Noble Sachawachiak, arctic knight, *sans peur et sans reproche*, who, despite all the evil he had suffered at the hands of the white man at Point Barrow, was still prepared to help those of the whites he considered his friends, as he had already done in the past.

Four or five sledges stood ready loaded on the ice beside the ship with thirty or forty dogs jerking and tugging at the traces, howling and barking, snapping at each other, biting so that they drew blood, disregarding our stern shouts and yelping when the stinging whip-lash caught them.

We were off! All the Eskimoes turned out to see us set out to-wards—well, they all thought we were going to our deaths; we, that we were going to the unknown land. They stood there freezing in the biting cold, and, when the sledges began to slide across the crunching snow with every lashing and every joint creaking, they called out their farewells. The air was full of good advice and ad-monitions to be careful, and among it all the more restrained 'Good lucks' of the companions we were leaving behind.

At last we were on our way!

As soon as we had got beyond the land and saw the unbroken horizon of ice in the north we came in among a hell of ice. The shoeing was stripped off the runners of the sledges, and the sharp ice tore great splinters out of the runners themselves, cut the dogs' pads till they bled, so that a trail of splinters of wood and gory paw-marks marked our laborious path across that dreadful crushed ice which occupied the two or three miles between the permanent land-ice and the drifting mass of pack-ice.

Our heavily laden sledges could not stand up to the violence of it and collapsed, but even so we got through and on to the pack-ice before things got too bad. And as we hoped that the worst was now over we scrapped the sledges we had and sent back across the living ice and the land-ice for the reserve sledges which we had wisely left behind for some such eventuality.

It was a good thing we had them, as otherwise we should have had to abandon our sledge-journey in the first few days; but by leaping from one bit of ice to the other, but using the momentary support of an unstable lump which spun round beneath our feet, by using a baby floe as a highly unsafe ferry to take us across narrow channels of water, by leaping and jumping like hares across the thick ice-gruel—we succeeded in a short time in getting our reserve sledges, and the return trip to the pack-ice with the empty sledges went comparatively easily.

71

We pitched tent on a large safe floe just on the other side of the land-channel, and there transferred our sledge-loads and said good-bye to some of our crew who had helped us across the difficult first stretch of ice and also to Sachawachiak, who was still trying to persuade us to abandon the idea. But he didn't know the stubbornness of the white man who, having once decided to do something, will try to carry it through whatever the consequences may be. And Sachawachiak shook his head sorrowfully and uncomprehendingly, gave us some more good advice and hurried across the crushed ice back to the firm, safe land-ice, from which he and his companions fired a farewell salute.

As far as Sachawachiak was concerned that was tantamount to a funeral salute over friends who had died, for a short time later when he met a missionary from Herschel Island, he told him that the three of us who had gone out into the pack-ice to find the unknown land, had perished there. The missionary passed this news on to a gold-digger who was going to Dawson City. That would have been bad enough, but the gold-digger improved on the story and made it more interesting by saying that he had spoken with an Eskimo, a very trustworthy man, who with his own eyes had seen us perish in the ice, but had himself managed to get back to land alive.

That had the right ring to it; it was news they could telegraph out from Dawson City, and thus it eventually reached Denmark, where for a year or more my father and mother suffered the agony of doubt over my presumed death.

For us, however, it was a wonderful feeling and a great relief to have reached the big floes where there was no danger that the ice at any moment might open out beneath our feet and plunge the sledge, and possibly us as well, into the icy water.

CHAPTER VII

IN THE PACK-ICE

We drift westwards—'Land' in the north—More rabies—Difficult sledging conditions—Ferrying across open leads—Difficult ice resembling land—Bear-hunting and stormy weather in the pack-ice

A GREAT calm settled over our little caravan after the others had left us. We could halt where we wished and take our time to find the best way through the pressure ridges which fringed the extensive icefields. We could pitch tent on ice several yards thick when tiredness got the better of us or of the dogs, or if the lash of the east wind was cutting too deep and causing frost-bite on noses and ears, piercing our furs so that it felt as if we were naked to the icy storm. That east wind harried us out there on the ice as it had already harried us on land and on the stretch we had already covered which had been neither land, sea nor proper ice.

Our joy at having at last found comparatively firm going was considerably tempered a couple of days later when the bearings we took on the land showed that we were drifting fast to the west with the ice which, according to the theories advanced earlier, should have been more or less stationary. That theory had been one of the proofs of the unknown land's existence, but it was now only too obvious that that proof did not hold water. Were we now, so early, to be forced to dismiss the evidence on which we had built many of our hopes?

The prospect was not good, but we took comfort by telling ourselves that we were still very near the land, and that perhaps the current would change when we got further out. We also cursed the fact that we could still see the mountains in the south and so be reminded of our westward drift every time we turned round.

Part of the ice we were sledging across was exactly as Captain Collins had described it: huge ice-floes many miles wide with hillocks and gullies much higher and deeper than we had experi-

73

enced in the tundra, twenty-five, often thirty-five feet, and not seldom even more, from the top of the hillock to the foot of the gully. That was a good sign, for such ice could not possibly have been formed in the open polar seas—so why worry further about the westward current?

One morning when Storkersen had emerged from the tent and rubbed the sleep from his eyes, he gave vent to a resounding cry which got Leffingwell and me out of our sleeping-bags quicker than ever before, for that excited cry was the same as that which throughout the ages has kindled joy in so many sailors' hearts and driven the sweat of fear from their foreheads: 'Land ahead!'

We ran up to the top of the nearest mound of ice and never felt the freezing wind though we stood there in clothes which were still clammy with the damp warmth of our sleeping bags.

What Storkersen had seen was certainly very like land, there was no doubt about that. Mountain tops blue in the distance, a long way off, or perhaps rather the billowing surface of an upland with long, rounded hills. And yet there was something wrong with that land, for never before had we seen hills so completely covered with snow and ice as those appeared to be. There wasn't one dark cliff face or shadow to be seen, not one black rock, just ice and snow. Could what we could see away there in the north beneath the glow of the morning sun really be just an illusion? Could that which so strikingly resembled land be only ice with raised slopes of the same kind as that on which we stood?

We could not make up our minds, but some hours later, when the sun's rays fell directly on to that vision of the promised land, we had to admit that it was an illusion: the rounded hills out there in the north were no longer bluish, but shining white! There was no doubt that it was ice, the heavy palaeocrystic ice which was also one of the proofs of the existence of land.

So it wasn't land we saw—not that time, and our disappointment after the initial overwhelming joy was naturally great. But disappointment can swiftly turn to joy, and you get used to disappointment when sledging, so we took it comparatively calmly, as we had the many disappointments which had preceded it, and as we would take all those which were bound to follow.

And we still believed in the land, the unknown land.

We encountered incessant difficulties with the pressure ridges which were either in the course of being formed where two floes were in collision under pressure of wind or current and being broken into lumps and pieces—or else disintegrating as two floes were released and drifting apart again.

It happened, happened over and over again, that huge blocks of ice heaved themselves up right under our sledges, as though they were living beings trying to bar our path, and not dead lumps of ice weighing many, perhaps even hundreds of tons.

And it happened, and also not infrequently, that we laboured hard to get across a ridge, only for it suddenly to come to life beneath our feet and disintegrate, because some change in the current was driving the floes apart. Then the huge blocks of ice would sink into the sea with great splashes, while we struggled for dear life with the dogs which were mad with fright, and the heavy sledges, trying to get them out and on to safe ice, or ice as safe as pack-ice can be, which is not saying a great deal.

At other times we sank into deep soft snow, often up to our waists, while the sledges stuck fast in the yielding mass in which neither the dogs nor we could get a firm footing. Even when we were getting on finely, and things looked promising, we could come to wide channels between the drifting ice-fields. For a short while we might find delight in the play of the sun-glitter on the little wavelets, and in the seals which inquisitively stuck their heads out of the water to see what had caused the shouts and cries and yelps that had broken the eternal hush of the pack-ice. But after that momentary delight we cursed these leads, across which we had to get ourselves one way or another.

It was not easy to get round them. To try could take us miles out of our course and perhaps waste a whole day's labour. The most attractive way was to get hold of a little ice floe and use it as a ferry, even though that was in a way equivalent to putting oneself into the power of unknown and rather hostile forces. Often things went as they should, and we got across the channel with sledges and dogs safe and sound: but sometimes our floe-ferry would slide gently out on to the sparkling water and while we rejoiced that soon we would be able to sledge on again across the large floes on the other side, it would suddenly halt for no reason that we could see, and we might have a long wait before we reached the floe which was our objective—or perhaps even be glad to be able to get back to that from which we had set out.

It was uncomfortable being the plaything of the capricious winds and currents, and it was also cold having to stand on a little ice-floe perhaps for hours on end waiting and wondering what it would take it into its head to do with us—perhaps twist round and round, or suddenly capsize for some unknown reason—we saw several of them do that while we were on safe ice, and thanked our lucky stars that we hadn't entrusted our lives and chattels to them.

We men are so made that we prefer to decide our speed and direction ourselves, and that we certainly did not do when we used an ice-floe as a ferry; so, after having struggled across a number of broad leads and become most heartily sick of floe-ferrying, we decided that sledging and sailing were cognate arts, and after that, when we came to a broad lead which had to be crossed, we unloaded one of the sledges and transformed it into a sort of lighter by wrapping a tarpaulin round it. Then one of us with a line tied round his waist and a spade in his hand as a paddle, would cautiously embark in that rather insecure craft, and paddle across the lead which was often more than a hundred yards broad, sometimes having to break a thin crust of ice in order to reach the opposite side, where he made the line fast to a piece of ice. Then we began cautiously hauling the sledge backwards and forwards; loaded on the outward trip and empty on the way back, time after time for hours on end, with our hearts in our mouths. When all went well, that was fine, and we nodded delightedly to each other as we transformed the lighter back into a sledge. But if ever things had not gone as we hoped, had we ever been unlucky enough to lose sledge and contents, then we might just as well have followed them into the depths, for to have managed without equipment and sledge, whether we toiled on towards the land in the north, or back the way we had come, was quite out of the question.

We had too the eternal east wind, often of storm strength, to contend with. It was a hard and merciless enemy which found every hole in our clothing and plunged its icy arrows deep into our bodies. That was bad enough, but what was still worse was that wind and current sent us so far and so quickly westwards that we had to change direction many times in order to keep heading north, with perhaps a little east, for that, we thought, was where we were most likely to find our promised land.

And every change of course meant that we had expended toil and provisions to no purpose.

Sledging had been hard from the first moment we set foot on the drifting ice. But hard or not, we progressed in one way or another, and in the beginning we had the advantage that we were unable to believe there could possibly be anything worse than what we were growing accustomed to regard as normal life on the pack-ice.

But there was, and we ought of course to have been prepared for it, but perhaps we had deliberately shut our eyes to the approaching and unavoidable disaster. This was the recrudescence of rabies, and that at a time when we could not manage without the dogs.

Our dogs had all appeared to be fit and well when we left Flaxman Island, but soon after we started sledging they began to show signs that the dreaded disease was about to break out again. After it had ravaged our pack that winter, we had with unjustifiable optimism thought we were rid of it. Perhaps its recurrence was brought on by the hard way the dogs had to toil by day and the harsh conditions they had at night, when they were compelled to sleep out in all weathers, with only a warming layer of snow to cover and shelter them from the wind at the best of times.

A couple of our dogs had died before we had been eight days on the ice. We used to wake in the night to hear mournful howls or hoarse barking and knew that yet another had been attacked by the filthy disease. Whilst we still had dogs enough to pull the sledges more or less adequately, we shot infected animals as soon as they displayed incontestable signs of rabies, but soon we had to stop doing that and let the infected dogs pull as long as they possibly could, for the sledges had to go forward.

That was very hard, for on these expeditions you make friends of your sledge dogs, and we disliked having to drive the poor brutes to the utmost. On such a trip, however, you cannot be soft, and there could be no question of sparing the dogs either toil or pain: either we had to abandon the idea of getting far enough from known land to be able to determine whether the unknown land existed or not, or else both dogs and men together must strive with all their might: and that we men did willingly, with the joy of a possible landfall our only and full reward; but the poor dogs had to be driven, and for them death was the only release from endless toil.

We toiled with the sledges so that we sweated despite the cold; each one of us pulled considerably more than even the strongest dog. From the moment we started in the grey twilight of day till we halted long after Venus had come out in the evening sky, we walked bent forward in the traces and pulled and pulled till things went black before our eyes, lifting the heavy sledge over sharp ice-blocks, urging the dogs with cries and cuts of the whip to give their utmost—and all the while searching out the best way through the huge masses of ice which the pressure of storm and current heaped up, now often even higher than before, and which could turn a stretch of good sledging surface into an impassable obstacle in a matter of minutes.

It was an all but hopeless labour, and whenever we had to call a short halt so that the dogs and we could have a breather, two of us had at once to go ahead and climb some eminence so as to get an idea of what sort of ice lay in front of us. Usually there was little comfort in the sight, but it would sometimes happen that one glance northward sent us hastening back to the sledges, shouting to the one who had remained with them, that there was splendid going some few hundred yards farther on. By the time we, hurrying breathlessly so as not to lose the least opportunity, had reached the sledges, he would have whipped the dogs out of their torpor, disentangled the traces and be moving off with the first sledge.

What a joy it was to reach those really big floes and sledge across them at a slow trot. We laughed to each other when we heard the soft crunch of the runners on frozen snow, or when we saw ice-crystals glinting and sparkling in the sunlight as though the ice were powdered with all the riches of the Orient: gleaming diamonds, glowing emeralds and rubies strewn upon that glittering white surface.

We could sledge for hours, sometimes for a whole day, perhaps even two days, through deep valleys with high ice-slopes to the east and west; we might find convenient dips in the slopes, low passes, when the direction of the valley changed so much that we could no longer follow it without going too far off our course towards the unknown land in the north. And when at last tiredness compelled us to call a halt, it was a real delight to be able to sit on the sledge with our faces turned towards the sun.

On such days it was a joy and a delight to be sledging towards our unknown goal; our mood would become softer and we would find time to fondle our dogs who, forgetting our stern shouts and the stinging lash, would press in close to us, giving little affectionate whimpers, sharing in the joy and peace they sensed around them. And then we would regret most horribly the harshness with which conditions had forced us to treat the poor dogs, which did their best to help us towards our goal—which for them meant only hunger, cold, suffering and in the end, death.

Hard is the lot of the sledge-dog.

And when the western sky glowed in the golden gleam of the sunset and the snow crystals absorbed the splendour of it, and became one with it, then we pitched tent with sixty or a hundred feet of ice between us and the ice-cold water, a safe and secure camp. That heavy ice, whose surface lay so high above that of the pack-ice that we often had difficulty in getting the sledges up on to it, was so like land that, if we hadn't known better, we would have believed that we had reached our goal, the unknown land—or rather, small islands off the coast of the land we had travelled so far to find. Yet, for all its resemblance to land that heavy ice drifted with wind and current like the pack-ice surrounding it, so land it could not be.

It took some little time to undo the frozen lashings on the sledges, to put up the tent and get the frozen canvas draped more or less along the ribs. But once the tent was up, it provided shelter for the one of us whose turn it was to make all as snug as possible, spread out the warming caribou skin over the cold ice, try to break the stiff-frozen sleeping bags open far enough for us to be able to shove our legs in, get the primus going and a pan of ice put over the flame in preparation for the undoubted highlight of our day, its one and only hot meal.

Meanwhile the other two would have enough to do with the outdoor jobs which always lay at the end of a day's toil: tether the dogs to long chains, feed them and see that everything else edible, including their harness and the whip, were put out of the reach of those omnivorous animals.

The tent with its warmth and steam and smell of food was a heaven to enter when at last the jobs were done, but it was only when we had wriggled right down into our sleeping bags, which were still so rigid that we literally had to break the ice binding the two sides together with our feet, that we could really enjoy it. And when the ice which had stuck the hair on the hide together in hard tufts at last melted and the moisture became warmed to body temperature, we would make an attempt to discuss the day's events while shovelling in our scalding pemmican, yet often we were so tired that we fell asleep before our bowls were empty.

If we had found one of those heavy, land-like floes to pitch tent on, we would not be disturbed by our ever-wakeful sub-

(*Above*) *Duchess of Bedford.*
(*Below*) On board *Duchess of Bedford*: Leffingwell, Ejnar Mikkelsen, Dr Howe, Ejnar Ditlevsen.

(*Above*) Ernest de Koven Leffingwell.
(*Below*) Meat skins hung up to dry.

consciousness as we were when we had to camp on ice that was not too safe, and so slept a good heavy sleep. It could happen that even this was disturbed by the dogs, and when their howling and frightened barking became so insistent that we had to shake ourselves awake and see what could have gone wrong in the big, white, cold world outside, we would drag ourselves out slowly and reluctantly.

We shrank from letting any of the damp warmth escape from our sleeping-bags, shrank even more from having to creep half way out of the warm sleeping-bag and have hoar-frost off the tent-cloth falling on our heads and necks, where it would melt and run in tiny streams down our bodies, right far down. Such melted rime was shudderingly cold, but most stimulating, and it sent us with numb fingers to undo the ties of the tent door which we opened only just sufficiently for us to be able to peer out into the light night and see if there was anything there to have frightened the dogs.

Often it was only one of the dogs which had had a bad dream and moaned so loudly that the others had woken up and expressed their sympathy for it in plaintive howls. Sometimes it could be a poor dog which could feel the first stage of rabies raging in its body, or perhaps the creaking of the ice had frightened one of them. And occasionally, by turning in its sleep one of the dogs threw the warm covering of snow off itself and became so bitterly cold that it had to give expression to its feelings at the misery of its lot.

But it also happened, and luckily quite often, that the dogs had good reason to call for help, when their frightened barking meant that that solitary roamer of the pack-ice, the great white polar bear, had winded the strange scent of our camp and had followed it until eventually he found himself standing outside the tent gazing at the tethered dogs which would be tearing and jerking at their short chains, howling and barking with fear or with longing for juicy bear's meat.

Then we in the tent would be wide awake in an instant; the tent door would be flung wide, we would seize the rifles which were always loaded, a shot or two would ring out, and the three of us would turn out to skin and quarter the dead bear, a mean job, cold and yet delightful at the same time, for it gave us an opportunity when the body was opened, to fumble for the guts with our frozen hands in the deliciously warm steaming blood which filled the dead beast's abdomen and chest. That was a much sought-after job, and one which also cleaned your hands for you.

When at last we had quartered the bear and each had received his due, the sledging trip seemed to be well worth while, and the rest of the night would be given over to an orgy of eating, both inside the tent and out. The primus roared; the frying, perhaps singeing, meat, filled the tent with greasy, choking fumes and smoke. And we ate and laughed, ate so that the juice of the meat ran down our beards and froze there. And how we enjoyed listening to the satisfied grunts of the dogs outside the tent. Then all would be forgotten in belching repletion, and men and dogs would relapse into a stupor.

After such a feed both men and dogs required a longer rest than we otherwise allowed ourselves, and when, as sometimes happened, during the orgy or just after, the wind got up, and began whistling in the guy-ropes and making the walls of the tent bulge, then we nodded to each other in satisfaction and crept still deeper into our warm sleeping-bags of caribou skin, enjoying the snugness of that narrow space and clasping mittens and stockings to our chests to dry them a bit before we had to put them on again, then, with a last effort, we pulled the bags shut over our heads so that no warm air could escape or any cold blast come in and, happy in our repletion, subsided deep into the land of dreams.

When your tent is pitched on safe ice, one day of storm can be most pleasant, but two is too many, even if you have a freshly shot bear to feast on. And if the storm lasts for three days, you just don't know what to do with yourself.

Outside the tent the drifting snow is swirling across the ice, and space, which otherwise seems boundless, has shrunk to a tiny white centre in the scurrying clouds which drive across the ice like a flood of milk. You have to go out now and then to see to the dogs, which as a rule gladly let themselves be snowed under with their noses covered by their bushy tails, and they are thoroughly happy like that, as long as the snow does not lie so thick and heavy on them that they are suffocated by it.

It does not take long before the little space inside the tent comes to feel like a prison and the sleeping-bags like clammy poultices. The snow under the tent melts, water makes its way through the coverings, which are supposed to be waterproof, and is sucked up into the sleeping-bags, making them even damper than before. You twist and turn in an effort to rest, to avoid too much moisture, and as tiredness is dispelled, you begin to grow anxious because of the lengthy inactivity, and groan and grunt as though trying to vie with the buffeting wind, and finally relapse into black despair: will the damned storm never stop?

It always did, of course, as we had known it would, but days when you are storm-bound can be mortally long. We used to look forward with longing to the time when we could dig our rested dogs out of their snowy lairs and drive them on northwards on the heels of our aspirations.

CHAPTER VIII

EARLY SUMMER ON THE PACK-ICE

Open water between the floes—Doubt of the island's existence—The deep Arctic Ocean—We give up the search—Sledging south for the coast of Alaska—Drifting out towards the open Arctic Ocean—Land at last—Back to our winter harbour

IF fate has so arranged it that you have to pitch tent on ice which is not very thick, your subconsciousness is perpetually at work: you are wide awake at the least sound which is not altogether usual and familiar, and you lie and listen, listen to the creaking and crunching of the ice, to its loud groans when it is struck by the ruthless lash of the frost, listen for the dogs, try to guess from the sounds what is happening out there on the insecure, thin ice.

Sometimes high above the howling of the wind a twang like that of a bowstring parting would suddenly ring out, and at once all three of us would be sitting up in our sleeping-bags listening and listening: Did you hear that? And, one night, after such a ominous twang the ice actually did split right under the tent, between two sleeping-bags, and before we had wriggled out and got clear of the toppling tent there was a gutter of open water a yard wide between the two sleeping-bags.

We had to hurry then; the tent was bundled together anyhow; our things brought to safety, the dogs freed from their chains and harnessed to the sledges and shortly afterwards we were moving, making for safer ice wherever we could find it in that wilderness, while all around us, wherever we looked, the ice was breaking and threatening us with destruction.

Those open leads form incredibly quickly once the ice has split under the pressure of a storm or heavier ice; and a thin floe can be split into bits and pieces in a very short space of time. Then, whichever way you go your way is barred by black water, across which somehow or other you have to get. It does not make things easier when the storm seizes you and your dogs in its grip and sends you and the sledges hurtling across the ice like an abandoned ship. The snow flies, pricking your face with its myriad needles, and stinging salt spray comes swirling from the open leads, and mist envelops you and blocks out the view, blinding you, and you fumble along without any idea where you are going or what you are going to encounter.

The dogs are frightened, halt abruptly at narrow leads which they could jump with ease, and which at any moment may suddenly become too wide for them to pass. They howl, recoil from the water which they have to cross, huddle together in senseless terror. And you call and shout, crack the whip, lash them with it, hard—for they *must* jump, you *must* get across and find slightly safer ice somewhere and that as soon as possible. To drive round helplessly on the breaking ice can only spell death.

Then at last you stumble on to a floe of thicker ice and can halt for a moment, get your breath—and you forget the beastly leads as all bad things are forgotten or mitigated once you have them behind you. And the next day, perhaps, the sun is shining again over a seemingly endless ice-floe, striking brilliant glints from the snow-crystals, and if you are also lucky enough to get a bear and are able to eat as much as you can put away, then sledging becomes a glorious thing once more.

So it was with us for a month, for the best part of two. We toiled northwards and the age-old floes grew bigger and bigger, so that often beginning and end could not be seen together; it was like sledging in extensive country with low hills and warm valleys. For it did become relatively warm as time passed and the sun got higher into the heavens. The snow became dull and almost lustreless, so wet and soft that the dogs sank into it, we sank into it, and the sledges sank into it up to their cross-pieces. Everything ran with moisture. Then, so determined to get on were we, we turned the light night with its crisp frost and hard snow into our day, and spent comfortable 'nights' in a tent which was light and bright, lit and warmed by the sun, so that we were able to sleep without our beards freezing to the thick hair on our caribou-skin sleeping-bags.

Such sledging really was a delight for body and soul. It all went so easily; the storms were tempered, and day after day our sharp sledge-tracks were drawn farther and farther north across the ice, following the migrant birds which winged their way past above us with loud chattering and gabbling to disappear swiftly into the blue expanse of the northern sky.

Why did the birds want to go there if there was no land?

We should then have been so far from the Alaskan coast that we ought to have been able to see the unknown land of legendary delights, if Harries' calculations were roughly correct.

But were they?

We were beginning to doubt, and often I found myself thinking of his last words to me on Washington railway station: 'Friend Mikkelsen, I believe the land is there. All night I worked through —' and then the rest was drowned in the noise, though I could guess what it was: '—my calculations and they are correct all right.'

Yes, if only that was so.

The observations of latitude we made each noon showed distinctly that we were daily coming farther north, that we should be roughly where the unknown land was calculated to lie. We took longitudinal observations whenever the sun was as it had to be for them, and calculated our longitude. Those calculations were disheartening, for unfortunately they showed that we were still drifting westwards, so far west that we were even beginning to look to the east for our land and not to the north as before.

Might that land still be there after all?

Doubt began to gnaw at us. Doubt took all pleasure out of the good progress we were making. Doubt paralysed our tongues each time we felt a desire to say something about the unknown land. Doubt kept us awake by day in our warm tent, and doubt rode with us at night on the sledges, weighing them down, so that we were almost unable to drive them on.

Many of our dogs had died, the rest were done up, exhausted wrecks. All our things were worn out: the sledges on the point of collapse, our skin-clothing in rags, and the petroleum we used for cooking was rapidly disappearing, the tin gurgling hollowly when we poured the precious stuff into the primus. Our provisions, too, were dwindling with appalling rapidity, both those for ourselves and the dogs' food which they had to have if they were to be able to stagger on. In fact, the outlook was far from good.

And that unknown land, what about it?

We no longer mentioned it; no one would put into words what each separately thought both early and late: we did not believe any more in their existence in that part of the Beaufort Sea. And each time our eyes fell on the half-empty, damaged sledges, another unutterable thought forced itself upon us: can we even manage to get back to the Alaskan coast with the few provisions we have, with exhausted dogs and sledges become so rickety that we felt it was a miracle they did not disintegrate each time we had to cross a ridge or a mere hump on the mile-wide floes. And would the current which kept taking us westwards—faster and faster, but perhaps that was just imagination—ever let us reach the land?

Our progress northwards became slower and slower. Doubt and the many queries it raised dragged at our feet like prisoners' fetters. Day and night it paralysed our thoughts and actions, and made a burdensome duty of what before had been a joy to do.

Things just could not go on like that, and my two companions kept looking at me with enquiring eyes. A decision had to be taken—and soon! And it was I who must say the first word.

It had to come, and it came, but it was hard to have to drop the traces, halt the crawling sledges and admit defeat, saying: 'This can't go on; let's say the things we are all thinking!'

We sat down on the sledges and got out the maps, marked our approximate position, measured—and looked at each other. It was a long way to Alaska, longer than the distance we had already covered, because we had drifted so far west that we would have extra distance to make up if we were to reach land—in the south now, not in the north.

We ought of course to have taken soundings to test whether we had come beyond the edge of the Continental shelf, out over deep water where it was improbable we would find land. But we had believed in the land in the north so firmly that it seemed unnecessary to take soundings when we had so much else to do.

But now we no longer believed in the land in the north, so now we could and should take a sounding. Down went the lead taking more and more of the thin line after it. Half had unwound and still the lead was dropping. The line ran out and out, until we had to start braking it in case we lost both lead and line. The line quivered with the tension.

With only thirty feet of line left and almost 6,500 feet out, I stopped the lead's swift plunge towards the bottom of the Beaufort Sea and looked at my two companions: 'Friends, our labours have been wasted, the risks have been in vain, all hope of finding new land is dead. We can no longer expect to find land here. Perhaps farther east, but not here. Let's haul the lead in again— if we can.'

It took an hour or so before we were able to straighten our aching backs and chuck the lead on to the sledge—and with that the dice were cast. Now we had to head for land, as hard as we could, for our lives in fact. Could we make any headway against that current? Could we get to the land before we drifted with the ice west of Point Barrow—out into the open Arctic Ocean, from which we should never be able to struggle back to Alaska's now so desirable coast?

An hour later we had removed from the sledges everything that was not absolutely essential, and when the midnight sun was shining enticingly in the north and the heavens and the ice were swathed in a golden-red glow, we cracked our long whips above the backs of our tired dogs and followed behind our own interminable long black shadows southwards towards the coast of Alaska some two hundred miles away.

It had cost us a lot to get out as far as we had, but we had had hope to help us, and that had got us over many difficulties. Now we had the additional burden of disappointment to carry, and it was appallingly heavy, paralysing both for our thoughts and our leaden limbs.

We remained silent for an hour or two, perhaps a whole day, I don't remember how long. I only remember the gloomy silence as we headed south, our black shadows showing us the way. The silence was not even broken by calls to the dogs which crept along without a sound, stupefied by our numbness; there wasn't even a crack of the whip to be heard.

But we were young, our spirits could be damped for a time, but not broken—and then it was also conceivable that that damned unexpected current had taken us west of the land and that perhaps this was lying hidden behind the ice in the east. And there would be another spring coming, and perhaps it would be possible to scrape enough equipment together so that we could go out into the ice again and search for the land elsewhere among the great floes. It could hardly be more rigorous than what we had already come through, and our dogs would hardly be ravaged by rabies a second year running. Perhaps it would go better a second time!

Again a little flame of hope was kindled, slender enough to begin with, but it was fed every day and soon was burning with a quiet, heart-warming flame: all that ice, the thick and extensive floes so like land with their hills and valleys, must have a natural explanation, and *that* could only be that the ice had been halted for many, many years by land somewhere or other in the Beaufort Sea.

So then I was busied with plans again, and that made things easier, took the depression from my mind—and then we had achieved something by our arduous sledging across the pack-ice: we had already explored a large part of the Beaufort Sea and that naturally reduced the area in which we could look for the land, and also we had gained a lot of dearly bought experience which would benefit us the following year and lighten the toil of finding that well-hidden land in the uttermost north.

It is amazing how stimulating fresh plans can be to body and soul: we felt less tired as the plan took shape and our thoughts got busy; once more we were able to feel glad that at least we were alive, glad at the progress we were making towards land; now we could, and had to make use of all our strength and all our experience so as to reach the coast of Alaska as soon as possible in order to try again next year.

Once again we took an interest in the daily observations which showed our progress. We rejoiced over every mile of southing, but we were also worried by the fact that the great ice-floes were drifting westwards more quickly even than on our outward journey. The melting of the thinner ice, and the clearing up which the summer sun must have done between the floes, had evidently given the larger floes more room in which to move—unfortunately always towards the west or the north-west, while we had to get to the south-east in order to reach land before it became too late.

That was our great worry as we raced the drifting ice on our flight south: would we be able to reach land before we were carried past Point Barrow and out into the vast Arctic Ocean? If we could not, then presumably we would drift more or less along the same path as *Fram* had taken Fridtjof Nansen some years before, and in some three or four years' time our floe would reach the North Pole.

That was what would happen if we drifted beyond Point Barrow. We had as good as no provisions, no ammunition, no fuel, no good or warm clothing left; nothing to shelter us against the storms and cold of the approaching winter—in fact none of the things you must have to maintain life in that stern land even in the most wretched conditions.

It would be a grim outlook, if that happened, and there could be only the one outcome: within a month and a half at the most after passing Point Barrow we would have ceased to worry about anything. And if there was any comfort in that, it was certainly a meagre one.

The sledges were light, for we had almost no provisions left and had jettisoned our heavy winter equipment, which was either worn out or rendered superfluous by the warmer weather. Even so that hardly helped our progress, for the sledge-runners were so damaged and worn that they ran as heavily as if they had been shod with sand-paper and had to run over endless floes of more sand-paper. The dogs' strength dwindled from day to day, and so did their number. They were worn out; they died of exhaustion, some perhaps also of the dread rabies, which we now scarcely noticed. And when they were dead, their bodies and tormented flesh had to perform one last service and help to feed their surviving companions, providing food which had no strength in it, which only filled the dogs' stomachs without nourishing them.

How right Queen Alexandra had been: as patron of the RSPCA she could not also have been patron of our expedition. I realized that clearly every time my eyes fell on the lean dogs which slunk along with dull eyes, and tails between their legs, so exhausted that they no longer even wanted to snarl at each other, let alone snap, a mournful procession which only came to life when a bear was sighted and that bear was shot so that food could be had.

The outlook was not pleasant, but on the whole we did not think much about that, for all our thoughts, all our energies were concentrated on the one thing—to reach land before the current had carried us beyond it.

And we did it—as you almost always do, however great the risks. We reached the coast of Alaska after spending a good seventy days in that appalling pack-ice with its harsh moods, and with only three dogs alive out of the thirty or so which had been harnessed to our sledges when we left Flaxman Island.

It was glorious to have solid ground beneath our feet, to be able to laugh at such things as currents and storms and lack of provisions, for we had been lucky for once and had struck land some twenty miles east of Point Barrow at a place where a large family of Eskimoes had set up their tent for the summer.

And the Eskimo men had been successful in their hunting and fishing and kept the women busy, as we could see from the big fat salmon split and hung up to dry outside the tent, and from the amount of caribou meat which had been cut into strips and laid out on the shore to dry in the warm sunshine. Skins of seal and caribou were stretched out everywhere; and when we saw it we realized that we should be able to get all the food we could eat, and also new skin-clothes, or at least have the worst of the tears and holes in our old ones repaired.

The Eskimoes, however, refused to believe us when we told them from where we had come: 'from the ice in the north, from the land out there with the fat women? No, white men, you are lying like all whites. No one comes back from the ice and the land out there!' We could not convince them that we really had come from the ice. But the Eskimoes were perfectly polite about it: if for one reason or another we wished to say that we had been in the pack-ice out there, then by all means let us do so. But when they thought we weren't looking and glanced at each other, a smile quivered at the corners of their mouths and their eyes laughed: 'Queer white men. What was the point of telling such a lie?'

Ten days later we reached Flaxman Island. The Eskimoes there also wondered greatly, but they had seen us go out on to the ice, so they had no doubts on that score, but when they saw us return they were not at all sure that we weren't materialized evil spirits, the kind of *tupilak* which disappears on the pack-ice and strikes terror into everybody by coming and wailing and whimpering, by whining pitiably, when storms howl round the huts and people sit snugly indoors and are not to be enticed out into the bad weather.

It took quite a time before relations between them and the three of us became as frank and friendly as they had been before; and they never really liked being alone with us, though with others present they were more courageous.

Only Sachawachiak and Douglamana had no fears to try and hide; all they felt was joy that we really had come back from the ice, which till then had kept all who ventured out into it.

'And the land?' asked Sachawachiak, 'Did you see that?'

No, we told him, unfortunately we had seen no land. We must have been too far west. But the next year we were going to try again a bit farther east. Then we would find the land all right.

He just nodded, and stuck the point of his tongue through the labret holes in his cheek as he had a habit of doing when he was thinking deeply. 'Perhaps you are right; but you have no more dogs, so you'd better stay here.'

And Douglamana gave me an eloquent smile and said: 'Well, Miki, do you still believe the women out there to be so fat that you can't forget them?'

CHAPTER IX

SUMMER ON THE ALASKAN COAST

*Duchess of Bedford crushed by the ice—The crew have to return home—
Attempts to assemble another sledge party—Fateful results of a shot—
Herschel Island—A story of whaling—The Eskimoes' harsh circumstances
—Royal Mounted Police*

IT was of course a joy to have reached safe harbour again, but
otherwise we did not have so much to rejoice over, for during
our absence the *Duchess* had succumbed to the dread force of
the ice; she had been crushed in its iron embrace and mortally
wounded.

Our companions who had remained with her had been compelled by the water in her to move ashore; and, shortly afterwards,
when the masts went overboard because the keel had broken and
the hull all but dropped to pieces, they had salvaged material
enough from the wreck to build a house on the top of a little rise
not far from the Eskimoes' huts.

It was a big house and a good house, the largest on Flaxman
Island, but it was also a sad end to the lovely *Duchess of Bedford*
which we had sailed out from Victoria harbour with such high
hopes. The only reminder of past glories was a name-board on
which an anonymous carpenter in Victoria had carved and gilded
the letters: *Duchess of Bedford*. That they had salvaged and nailed
above the entrance to the house. In that moment of defeat,
penury and shipwreck, we were still able to honour the name of our
patron.

One day as I was standing looking at the house and the gilt
lettering on its name-board, one of the crew came up to me,
nodded at our home with its covering of tarred paper and said:
'There went our wages, Skipper, but never mind, the trip itself
has been worth the money.'

The others were of the same opinion, and so we could be just
as good friends as ever. But in the days which followed I could not

help noticing that their eyes were very often turned towards the mountains in the south, and that they had many long conversations with the Eskimoes about the best way to get to them. The gold country behind the mountains, perhaps in the mountains, was summoning them with its irresistible call.

Nor did I have any say in the matter. With the loss of *Duchess of Bedford* their obligations both to the ship and to me had come to an end, and they had so to speak paid for themselves with the loss of their outstanding wages.

When we had had a little time to get over the disappointments of our homecoming, I called my men together and explained to them that I wanted to make one more attempt to find the land out there, but starting from a point considerably to the east of where we were, roughly about Herschel Island. Would any of them like to come with me?

There was a long silence. Leffingwell had already told me to count him out. He was a geologist, and the mountains to the south had never been travelled by others than the Eskimoes, though it was doubtful whether even they had been there. That was where Leffingwell was wanting to go, and he thought that he should be able to do good work there.

Dr Howe had had more than enough of the ice during the first few days of the journey when he and Sachawachiak had helped us, and he wanted never to see it again. That was what the others also thought about it, and there was certainly no eagerness to accompany me out there again. Only Storkersen said nothing. Had he perhaps come under the spell, was his urge for adventure strong enough to lure him out on to the pack-ice again to search for the unknown land?

I saw the struggle going on in him, while he gazed at the map lying on the table between us; he seemed to be measuring by eye how far we would have to sledge across the ice before we could perhaps reach land, and weighing up how much it would cost in toil and risk to get so far.

Then suddenly he took his decision, looked up at me, brushed a

95

straggle of hair off his brow, and said: 'All right, Skipper, I'm
your man! If you go, I shan't hold back. It can't be much worse
next time than it was last.'

That was a relief. He was a good man to be with, that Norwegian, whom I had signed on in Victoria, by sheer chance,
and I was glad he had said that he would stand by me. Perhaps, in
spite of everything, I should be able to find an Eskimo to make a
third, or even one of the white men who were trying their luck
up at Herschel Island.

And equipment? Well, yes, but we didn't need to worry about
that at the moment. We had enough provisions for four or five,
and we would be able to get more in a short while when the coming
of the whaling fleet from the west announced the arrival of summer. And even if the ships could not get through the ice, as had
happened the previous year, we would still manage all right, for
we had learned a lot of things from that long sledge journey and
from living with the Eskimoes, which together meant a great deal.
One thing we felt certain of: where Eskimoes could manage, we
too must be able to exist.

So it was decided that we should try once again. The land
beyond the wilderness of ice still lured us.

Summer was upon us before we realized it, and with it came
Vilhjalmur Stefansson, a comrade in our venture, who had taken
his own route and come down the Mackenzie River to join us
that way. Stefansson was an archaeologist, and at Herschel Island
he had found conditions which interested him and made him
want to stay there. He had now come—more or less just to tell us
that he was leaving us again. The thing was that while at Herschel
Island he had met some Eskimoes who had come there from farther
east and it had struck him that they were lighter in complexion
than most Eskimoes were. He thought that they might have some
of Franklin's men for their forebears, or perhaps even the old
Norsemen from Greenland!

Stefansson called them 'blond Eskimoes.' It sounded most sensational, and had to be exploited. This Stefansson felt his previous

(*Above*) Sachawachiak.
(*Below*) Our house on Flaxman Island built from the wreck of *Duchess of Bedford*.

Looking for a possible way through the ice.

obligation would still allow him to do, and he did it. It must be admitted that we were in no position to do anything for him other than what we had already done by dragging him away from his previous plans for ethnographic work, I believe in Africa, and turning his attention to this work on the Eskimoes and the Arctic countries, subjects which he has exploited to the full. In the decades that were to come, one heard quite frequently of Stefansson's doings in the Far North.

It was in a way a good thing that Stefansson did not stay long with us, for the summer was short and much had to be done before winter came.

In the first place, the men whom the loss of the ship had rendered superfluous had to be sent home in the best available way. I didn't like their idea of going on foot across the mountains to the gold country in the south. That was far too dangerous; for these men were the substitutes we had got off *Thetis* that day in Jabbertown roads and they were too inexperienced, and too little was known about the country. Where were the passes through the mountains? What were they like? And how dangerous were they? Even the Eskimoes didn't know them, and as the summer advanced it made it more and more difficult to get southwards: the tundra was streaming with water and almost impossible to cross; and each time we paused to listen to the voice of Nature it had as an incessant accompaniment the rush of swift brooks and streams, all coming from the glaciers on the mountain slopes to the south.

Such a trip could never come off; the men's way home had to be by way of Point Barrow where presumably we should find a ship which would take them to safer parts in America. And so we started off in a company of three boats, toiling at the oars and sailing along gaily across the smooth surface of the lagoons when the wind was right. It looked like being a quick and easy journey, there wasn't a sign to be seen of all the ice with which we had had to contend the summer before. The sea was free of ice, as it usually is—but just not that year when we had so badly needed open water.

At one place we went ashore to shoot duck and geese, as we needed a little fresh food for the journey. We shot as many as would last us for two or three days and were getting ready to start off again, were ready in fact—when a shot rang out, then a cry, and Storkersen collapsed in the stern-sheets of his dinghy. He had forgotten to unload his shotgun; the hammer had been at cock and, as he was fumbling to get the gun stowed away, the inevitable had happened, and it had gone off and shot him in the foot. He had a toe or two broken, and the pain was considerable.

I realized at once how fateful that shot could prove for my intended journey across the ice the following spring, for I could scarcely make the attempt without Storkersen. However, when he had got over the initial scare and the pain had subsided a bit, he announced that he was still prepared to make the attempt with me, provided his foot recovered and did not become a hindrance. We had of course to turn back, and wait for the foot to heal.

As time went on I began to feel less certain of Storkersen. His interest in another sledge-journey across the pack-ice seemed to cool as the summer advanced and getting home became more and more possible; but I could hardly imagine that he would go back on our arrangement, if he recovered. Dr Howe had every hope that he would, and even a layman could see that the wound was healing quickly. By a couple of weeks after the accident, I had ceased to think much about it; if I did, it was rather to wonder how such a stupid thing could ever have happened.

At the beginning of August, when the whalers reached Flaxman Island, we received a number of parcels of provisions and equipment which friends had sent when they heard of the difficulties we had encountered with the ice the previous summer. That made everything much easier. Now, with a little economy, we could manage another sledge journey.

The whalers agreed to take our men home with them on their return, so after that there was nothing more for me to do at Flaxman Island, and as Storkersen's foot was continually improving, I was able to go aboard one of the whalers with an easy mind and sail with her to Herschel Island, where I hoped to be able to find a third man for the sledge journey—by all accounts there should be quite a number who might be suitable.

It was like coming to a proper town again, when we anchored in the splendid harbour at Herschel Island. A crowd of whites and Eskimoes had come to greet the first ship of the year. There were plenty of memorials to the great days of the past: both the many large warehouses which now were empty and tumbledown, and the smaller houses in which the whalers had lived during the short period when the seas there had swarmed with whales.

My arrival was even something of a sensation for the good people of Herschel Island, for they had heard the rumour that we had perished in the pack-ice, in fact it was there that the rumour had been embellished with so many credible details that it had seemed such good 'news' that one man had even thought it worth while to sledge four hundred miles across the tundra and mountains to take the story to Dawson City, where he sold it for what it was worth, thereby causing sorrow to more than one of our families. And there I suddenly was, an incontrovertible denial of the rumour, asking naively if any of the young men would like to go with me on another attempt to find the unknown land in the pack-ice.

My enquiry did not produce many applicants, for most no doubt considered such a sledge journey sheer madness, and I could not very well contradict them, though I did not regard it as quite so risky and stupid as others evidently thought it.

Those young men, I found, no longer had the drive which characterized the men of Herschel Island around 1895, which was when Little Joe had arrived. Little Joe was an enterprising trader from Point Hope, where one day he had loaded his little whaleboat with all the trade-goods he could scrape together in a hurry and sailed off in search of pastures new, a sudden departure necessitated by his having shot a companion in a drinking bout. He was fleeing from retribution and sailed alone northwards along the coast and eventually reached Herschel Island, a more or less unknown place, or at least known to only a few sealers, where he thought he ought to be safe from the sword of vengeance.

He remained on Herschel Island for a year or so, and then returned to Point Hope as a big man among the whalers, and to him all things were forgiven, for his boat was filled with precious furs, and he was also able to tell them that whales were so thick in the waters round Herschel Island that a boat could hardly get along because of them.

That sounded just the thing, and in the following years whalers and people of many kinds flocked to Herschel Island: large, steam-driven whaling ships with crews of fifty men or more, or small whaling sloops with Eskimo crews. Adventurers came from near and far, anticipating fine fishing in those troubled waters and hoping to find their bonanza in that remote part of the world. And there also came those who were only looking for a place where they could behave as suited them best, become rich by robbery and theft, if that would hasten on their goal, or also merely because they wished for unbridled debauchery and dissipation in which no one would interfere.

Around the turn of the century there were a dozen big whaling-ships wintering at Herschel Island, and that meant five or six hundred men to drink and fight, drawing knives or revolvers, whichever lay to hand. All these white men and the things they possessed attracted the Eskimoes from far and near like a powerful magnet: the men to do the work the whites would not be bothered to do themselves, the women to amuse the white men and help pass the time in the long winter. And the men were given spirits, the women too, as well as sparkling imitation jewellery, fine dresses and all sorts of feminine fripperies such as had never before been seen in that remote corner of the world, which in the eyes of the easily enticed Eskimoes became a paradise and a good place to live.

The whaling companies erected great warehouses for all the provisions, equipment and coal which the boats of the whaling fleet needed, pouring money into the place. A club house was built for the older whalers and small houses for those who preferred comparative solitude to living on board the overcrowded ships in winter quarters. Both on board the ships and in the small houses on the flat shore of Herschel Island the Eskimo women lived a glorious life, drinking themselves senseless with their white masters or with their fellow Eskimoes when the whites were elsewhere: with whom did not matter as long as they could get spirits and the desirable things the white traders offered for sale in such abundance.

Some missionaries in America heard of the Eskimoes' distress and of the licentiousness of the white men, and they sledged great distances across the tundra in the hope of being able to help the Eskimoes who so badly needed support and assistance; also perhaps in the vain expectation of being able to subdue a little of the white man's vitality.

But the missionaries were unable to do anything. Some left again after a short time there, disappointed by the Eskimoes' folly and lack of sympathy for the Christian doctrine and morality, of which the Eskimoes, of course, had never heard a word before, and bitter against their fellow-countrymen who had just laughed at their well-intentioned attempts and made fools of them. Others stayed and vainly tried to stop the rot which was leading the silly credulous Eskimoes to their destruction.

The missionaries' good example and pious exhortations were of no avail against the spirits the whalers provided and the goods which the Eskimoes coveted. The churches they had built in haste stood empty, or were only attended by a few of the infirm who were no longer able to take part in the debauchery and love-making of the whites and Eskimoes, yet who still listened longingly to the drunken noisiness of it during the twenty-four-hour long day or the month-long night.

And some of the missionaries ended up like the other whites on Herschel Island, and in a short time paved a good bit of the way to hell which is made practicable with good intentions.

The wildness of life on Herschel Island echoed far and wide, and then one day a dozen grim men in red tunics arrived at that island on the fringe of the Arctic Ocean. A detachment of the Canadian Royal Mounted Police had come to establish order and enforce respect for human life and the individual.

These men of the Mounted Police hit hard and recognized no difference between white man and Eskimo. They forbade the giving or selling of spirits to the natives, a thing which was illegal according to Canadian law, and those who would not listen had to be made to feel: both giver and recipient went to jail.

The white men were furious. They had only just found that nice remote spot where they could be free of that sort of intrusive prying, and now here these damned Mounties had come and were sticking their noses into everything.

And the Eskimoes too wondered. They had all been having such a good time, so they thought, and then these stern men had come, white like the others, yet they refused to give the Eskimoes spirits or to accept the favours of their women. These were peculiar men, of a kind they had not met before. And perhaps the strangest thing of all was that the other white men, whom the Eskimoes had previously looked upon as their undisputed masters on land and sea, whose word had been law to them and all others there, had grown so submissive towards the stern men in the red tunics, who even dared knock down those who caused disturbances, stole or killed people, before they took them away to some tiny little rooms with a little hole for a window and a thick door which was fastened with a stout lock.

And when next the Eskimoes met these white men who had been shut up for a while, they had become strangely quiet in their behaviour. Now and again one of the red-coated men would leave Herschel Island and with him would go a man who had killed another. And the red-coated man would come back but the other never did.

It must have seemed strange to the free-born Eskimoes, both men and women, who had never before known a superior with the authority and power to command, to see all these whalers, from the skippers to the ship's boys, being cowed in a short time by these few quiet men in uniform, who could give a friendly smile when all was peaceable and quiet, but whose eyes would flash with anger when drink had made the white man take liberties, and who always appeared when fighting broke out or shots were being fired, and would calmly go up to a man with a bloody dagger or smoking revolver in his hand and say to him: 'Come along with me!'

These men in uniform were incontestably masters of the Eskimoes' previous masters, and the Eskimoes wondered. It was not till long afterwards that they understood that these stern, grave men, who were always ready to help where help was needed, had more behind them than just courage and stern voices, that they were the representatives of an ordered society come to the lawless North, where they acted and gave orders by virtue of the power which stands behind all who enforce justice and the law.

Before a year had passed the Mounties had brought quiet and order to Herschel Island. In this they found an unexpected ally in the whalers themselves, who, in their frantic hunt after the precious whale, had driven it from the waters round the island, so that the whalers had had to spread out across the sea to the east in order to find them.

The whale adventure at Herschel Island lasted a decade; but after that it was over for good, and all that remained were the empty warehouses. The many little houses in which the whalers had lived during the winter were then occupied by the Eskimoes, a people ravaged by disease and avid for spirits, who only dreamed of the vanished merry days when life was easy and joyous and required none of the labour it now called for.

When I came to the island in the summer of 1907, there were lots of half-breed children everywhere. There were also some young men and women whose whaler-fathers—that must in fairness be said for them—had tried to give them an education by sending them to the schools for half-breeds in Unalaska. They had now come back to the country of their mothers and were neither Eskimoes nor whites. They had learned quite a lot, and some of them became missionaries of a sort, others teachers for the rising generation; most, however, became nothing at all, they were just stuffed with false ideas about life outside Alaska, and, poor devils almost all of them, condemned to live both then and for the future in that stern land without having learned the technique of hunting when they were children. Most lived on the borderline of starvation, and died early deaths which were hastened by the diseases that were their only inheritance from their fathers.

Far along the coast both to the east and west of Herschel Island you find deserted dwellings, grim monuments to the thousands of Eskimoes who, in their ignorance and desire for fun and spirits, had been drawn away to Herschel Island and there perished during the few bad years of the whalers' misrule.

The stern men were still on Herschel Island, no longer in red tunics, for that visible symbol of the law's authority was required no more, but dressed like the other white men, or like the Eskimoes. Only on public holidays did they appear in red. Their stern expressions had grown milder with the work of mercy they now performed as advisers and helpers of those children of Nature whom the white man had seduced. They were trying to heal some of the deep wounds which thoughtless and undisciplined white men had inflicted on the defenceless inhabitants of Herschel Island and its surroundings.

I lived in one of the barracks which the Mounted Police occupied. They were mounted no longer, but expert sledge-drivers with well-trained dog-teams. I asked them, for they knew all the men on the coast, which of the whites on Herschel Island they thought I might get to go with me into the pack-ice the following year.

They thought that it would be pretty difficult to find a suitable man, but that there was a young Swede on the island, called Axel Anderson, whom I might perhaps use if he would go, though that they rather doubted.

I went to Axel, told him about our recent arduous sledge journey in search of the unknown land, and asked him if he would make a third on a fresh attempt.

Axel was big and strong, but I was not so certain that he had sufficient guts to endure all the things which might happen to those who sledge on the pack-ice, nor was the chief of the Mounted Police, though he knew Axel quite well. There was a weakness about his mouth which I did not like.

But he was the only one who was in the least interested in the suggestion, and that made it easier to decide on him than if there had been many to choose from. So, the Swede Axel, Anderson and I shook hands on it that, together with the Norwegian, Storker Storkersen, we would journey out by sledge in the spring of 1908 to make a further attempt to find the unknown land.

CHAPTER X

A BITTER DECISION

I am let down—The sledge trip has to be abandoned for good—I want to get south to reach an ice-free harbour—A sledge-trip of either 700 or more than 2,000 miles—I choose the longer route

I ARRIVED back at Flaxman Island in the middle of one night late in September. Off I went, stumbling in the dark across the ground towards our hut, all eagerness to tell Leffingwell and Storkersen about my arrangements for the coming year. The frost was hard and the grass had frozen together into large tufts, nasty and dangerous to tread on, for it hurt to do so, and a twisted ankle could easily result from an incautious step. But, what was worse, the water-holes, of which there were many on Flaxman Island, had frozen over without the ice being thick enough yet to bear. Time after time my foot went through, and I plunged into freezing water, while the sharp ice flayed my trousers and cut the skin on my shins to strips.

I was spurred on by the successful outcome of my trip to Herschel Island and by wanting to surprise my friends by walking in and saying: 'Well, we start again in March!' At last I saw the patch of denser blackness in the dark which I knew must be our hut, I felt my way along the wall, found the door and was home.

It was so quiet inside, so unnaturally quiet and dark, that it felt rather as if I had somehow or other strayed into a burial mound. It was almost uncanny. But then I heard the deep, peaceful breathing of a man asleep. That was a relief, and I was just about to call out: 'Rise and shine!' when I choked the words back, held my breath and listened, listened intently into the darkness: there ought to be two men asleep there, and I could only hear one. I ought to be able to hear the other as well.

So I listened, yet judging by the sound that there was only one man in the hut. I groped my way to the bunks, struck a match and the light fell on Leffingwell sleeping there securely. Storkersen's bunk was empty and had not been used for some time, for it was also empty of all the little things which show that an empty bunk is nevertheless in use.

An icy sensation of having been let down and abandoned came over me, and it required an effort before I could wake Leffingwell and say: 'Where's Storkersen?'

'Gone,' he said, when he had come to his senses, 'he went south with the others a fortnight ago!'

I sat down heavily on a packing case. So I was back again where I had been! The expedition into the pack-ice must be abandoned, for I could not, dared not, go with Axel alone. And Axel would certainly not go with me, now that Storkersen had let us down.

'And his foot?' I asked.

That had been quite all right, I was told. The doctor had said that there was absolutely nothing to prevent Storkersen undergoing the hardships of the ice again. But Storkersen had not wanted to go any more. Leffingwell had tried to persuade him, but all his efforts were in vain. Storkersen had just kept on repeating: 'Yes, the foot's all right, but I just won't go out on to the damned ice again!'

That was a long and a difficult night to get through. My hopes had all collapsed round me; I should never find the unknown land.

And Storkersen? What had happened to make him alter his decision to go with me on to the ice—provided his foot was healed?

Leffingwell did not understand it either. Time after time, after I had left for Herschel Island, Storkersen had assured Leffingwell that he would loyally stick to his promise and go with me on to the ice in the spring. But then one day he had come back by himself from a part of the island where he and the others used to go and keep a look out for the ship which was to take them home, and without any preliminaries had told Leffingwell that there was no use us demanding that he fulfil his promise and go with me. If we did, he would sledge to Herschel Island with one of the natives and stay there. But under no circumstances would he go on to the ice.

'And I don't think he ever wanted to,' said Leffingwell. 'It was in pretty peculiar circumstances he got shot in the leg. Could he have shot himself on purpose in order to get out of it?'

Perhaps, and then I remembered one or two little things which could also have pointed to that being the case. Yet I could not conceive how he, the good companion, the bold team-driver, the light-hearted Storkersen, could have failed me so utterly and deliberately.

Yet that is what he had done: gone south with the others, let me down, and the sledge-journey must now be abandoned, unless Leffingwell—'Listen, Ernest, can I not persuade you to make another trip on the ice?'

'No, Miki,' he replied gravely. 'I knew you would ask that, and I have thought and thought it over many a time. But I can't. Your work is on the ice, mine on land, and I can't give mine up. Also I no longer believe in the land out there, and I hate the pack-ice.'

That was no news to me, and I could sympathize with his point of view: his work as a geologist, his very future perhaps, depended on what he could find in the mountains there to the south—not on the hypothetical land out there in the north. And when he no longer believed in that land's existence, there was no expecting him to sacrifice more for it than he had already done. And besides, he had long since said that he wouldn't go—even before Storkersen had said that he would.

While the night ran out and the pale autumnal sun rose and sent its rays in through the little panes of our hut, we talked the matter over and over without being able to reach any other result than that the sledge journey must be abandoned, unless Sacha-wachiak would be the third and come with us? I supposed I could rely on Axel?

Perhaps, but I didn't know. I no longer relied on anyone or anything. So I went to ask Sachawachiak if he would come, though I was pretty sure of his answer, and it was the refusal I had expected. Douglamana and the children held him back. 'If I went with you,' said the good fellow, 'and we stayed out there as I believe we would, even though you came back last time, Doug-lamana and the children would suffer. No, Miki, I can't go with you on to the ice.'

Axel Anderson, who reached Flaxman Island some days later, was obviously relieved and decided that he didn't wish to go either. 'If Storkersen has done a bunk and Leffingwell has had enough of the pack-ice, then I shan't go either,' he declared. 'And I'm not breaking a promise either, my promise was to go with you and Storkersen. With him gone, you've no claim on me.'

He was right, Leffingwell was right, and Sachawachiak too was right. My journey across the pack-ice in the spring of 1908 must be abandoned.

But what then?

My troubled mind began to bestir itself now that all hope of a sledge journey across the pack-ice was gone. I could not envisage a whole year's inactivity. Leffingwell could do his work by himself with Axel as assistant, and he would not hear of my staying behind just for his sake.

But what was I to do? We were well into October, and the last whaling ship had long since gone, so how could I get back into the great world where all things could happen?

Sledge, of course! That was the only solution. I must manage by myself one way or another. And even that might be rigorous enough. The maps were got out and I examined them carefully, such as they were, which was not very good. And I measured with the dividers. Even though I had known it would be a long way, the result made me hesitate. I had not thought it would be quite such a distance. It was almost impossibly far.

There were only two possibilities to choose between: either straight across the Alaskan peninsula to some open harbour far to the south, a sledge journey of a good seven hundred miles, or else along the coast, first to Point Barrow, then southwards to the Yukon River and on to an open harbour somewhere or other. But that would be a very long way: at least 2,300 miles.

The difference in distance was tremendous. Even seven hundred miles is a long way, when you have to walk every mile and also have a sledge to struggle with and tired dogs to drive forward. And the second route was more than three times as long—three times as many steps to be taken, three times the toil. The difference was enormous.

Leffingwell and I sat bowed over the map and tried to read from it what difficulties the route across the mountains would entail. It looked as though they would not be few. The mountains inland had obviously been delineated by a very imaginative cartographer. It was even impossible to reconcile the map with what we could see of the mountains; and so far as we knew no white man had yet got across the mountains, so where had the cartographer got his knowledge from? And no Eskimo we knew had been so far in among those great mountains in the south that he could tell us where the passes lay.

It didn't look at all a promising route. Where the Eskimoes had been in among the mountains while hunting the shy mountain goats, they had had to contend with violent storms, furious buffeting winds which they could not stand up to. Drifting snow would make sledging very hard, perhaps impossible, and nobody, either white man or Eskimo, lived there among the mountains, so that, if I chose that route, I would have to rely entirely and solely on myself, and so many unforeseen things could happen. No, that route was hardly practicable, even though it was nearly fifteen hundred miles shorter than the other. That factor weighed very heavily in the scale, but yet I decided against the mountain route and chose the longer, the very much longer way. The latter would mean sledging on sea ice, and I knew what that involved. I knew all about that and thought I could deal with it as well as anyone.

The journey along the coast was obviously perfectly practicable, but it was a long way, and it called for hard sledging to cover all those hundreds of miles before the warmth of the spring sunshine melted all the snow off the ground in the south; however, if I wanted to get to a steamer in some open harbour on the southern coast of the Alaskan peninsula, I just had to pay the price, and that was a sledge journey of 2,300 miles and more.

After the doubt and irresolution it was a relief to have taken a decision, even though I felt that I should probably regret it many a time when storms were howling, snow swirling and provisions short. But I was sure that I would have regretted it even more if I had decided to live in comparative comfort on Flaxman Island with the pack-ice for my neighbour and no means of sledging across it in search of the land which I had so hoped to find.

One sunny afternoon, after my decision was taken and the time for me to go was near, I walked out to the channel of open water which separated the pack from the land-ice, found the tallest pile of ice and clambered up to the top of it, and there I sat, wrapped in my warm skins, and had a last look across the pack-ice, saying goodbye to it and to the unknown land in which I still believed.

I reviewed in my mind everything which could have been an indication of its existence and longed to be out on the tempting ice, even though I had to admit to myself that our first sledge journey there had been dreadfully hard and that the next would presumably have been even harder.

My thoughts also went to all those who had shown confidence in me, and who had made it possible for me to go and look for that land, whether by their encouragement or their financial support. I had done everything possible to fulfil my moral obligations to those who had relied on me, but circumstances had been too much for me, the difficulties too great, the ice too intractable for the little *Duchess of Bedford*. There, after an hour's wrestling with all sorts of bitter thoughts, I said farewell to the hopes and expectations of several years and walked back in the sunset to the house on Flaxman Island. I must leave it to others to solve the mysteries of the Beaufort Sea.

CHAPTER XI

THE LONG, LONG JOURNEY

Farewell to companions and a hope—Hard sledging—Fires at night—
The expectations, disappointments and sufferings of sledge-dogs—Helpful
and hospitable Eskimoes—Too much hospitality

EVERYTHING was ready for my journey, and I had to start if I was to have any hope of getting through to open water south of the Alaskan peninsula before the spring sun made sledging impossible and compelled me to spend the summer somewhere in that desolate country.

Our Eskimo friends arrived early to say goodbye and wish me good luck on my long trip, and I was very glad to see them, but nonetheless Leffingwell and I felt the need of a little privacy, and behind a little hill of ice we found a corner sheltered from the biting north wind where the sun shone straight in at us. It was really warm there, and we sat down on a hump of ice to say goodbye, goodbye and thanks for five or six years of friendship and collaboration.

From the moment we had given each other our hands on it that we would sledge across the ice of the Beaufort Sea in order to find the unknown land which we both thought lay hidden there, we had looked with the same eyes upon things and events. We had toiled together without a murmur, together we had endured hard times both before we got started and on the long journey itself, and we had also shared disappointments in plenty; yet never had there been an angry word between us, and I am certain that not even in our thoughts had we ever criticized each other's arrangements, different though we were.

And now it was all over. Leffingwell was going inland to the distant mountains in the south to investigate them and the intervening tundra—where he found oil, not great gushing oil-geysers, yet enough for it now to be considered a very welcome reserve in

(*Above*) 'Shore Line' of age-old ice which can easily be mistaken for land.
(*Below*) Lunch on the pack-ice. Leffingwell and Storkersen.

(*Above*) Difficult going for sledges.
(*Below*) Sledge being used as a ferry across a wide lead.

view of the enormous consumption which will be required in the future to keep militarized Alaska going. And I—I was off by myself to follow the coast round to some open port somewhere over a couple of thousand miles away—heading for new travels, fresh adventures, going to meet such joys and sorrows as would come my way, perhaps also to face criticism for having spent a great deal of money without finding the land I had so loudly proclaimed must be there in the Beaufort Sea.

And it hadn't been there, or we hadn't found it, which amounted to the same thing as far as we were concerned. And though we had had to admit defeat, I was convinced that in the years to come others would have the good fortune to solve the mystery which the Beaufort Sea seemed to contain—and that made it no easier.

We said goodbye to each other on 15 October 1907, in that warm sunny corner behind a little hillock of ice, and when we met again forty-six years later, the first thing Leffingwell said to me was: 'Miki, the US Air Corps ought to invite you for a trip to Fletcher Island, for it was that, or its predecessor, which we were out after in the days of our youth.'

A few clouds were coming up from the south; the sun disappeared; it was getting late, and I had to be off, together with Axel, who was coming south with me as far as Point Barrow. I whipped up my few dogs and took the first of the many, many thousands of steps which I would have to take before my eyes could be gladdened by the sight of the open water a-glitter with sunlight along the distant coast of southern Alaska.

My dogs were not particularly willing and moved reluctantly; they were slow to get going, but after a lot of shouting, calling, barking and snarling we got started and headed westwards, while Ernest de Koven Leffingwell stood up on top of the ice hill, the hood of his anorak blown off his head and his long black hair fluttering in the wind, shouting and waving until we could neither hear nor see him. So the two of us trudged along at the side of the sledge, whip in hand, the trace over our shoulders, bent forward, as we hauled with all our might to help the dogs, two of whom were veterans from the pack-ice, the other three just big puppies; it was a poor team, but all the rabies had left us.

Even that trip was hard and laborious, but so all sledging is, so why say more about it. Sledging and inhuman toil—though not unmixed with delights—go together. If you want the former, you must also take the latter and lump it. Even so, springtime sledging with the ice thick and reliable is like a dance compared with the toil of sledging in the autumn. For, however cold it may be, it always takes time before the ice becomes properly hard, and until then it is thin and permeated with sea salt which forms beautiful flower patterns on the surface, and can give those with a speculative turn of mind material for all sorts of reflections on the combination: ice-flower-motif-salt, but which cause the ordinary team-driver to endanger his soul with all the oaths and curses he pours upon it with every justification.

The salt acts on a sledge like a sea anchor on a boat in distress at sea. It is almost impossible to pull a sledge through the salt slush, which forces its way through the thin soles of your *kamiks*, freezes your feet and makes frost-bite so probable that you will be very lucky if you escape it.

And ten times accursed is such ice if you have to pitch tent on it at night, for your sleeping-bag acts like a sponge and sucks to itself all the salt wetness on the surface of the ice, making the chittering person inside it feel as though he were lying in a wet poultice of freezing brine. And, what is even less pleasant, it is always a toss-up whether the thin salt-saturated ice will bear all night or not, especially when a storm is sweeping across land and sea, as is so often the case in the autumn.

You must avoid that thin salty ice, avoid it like the plague and take to sledging on land whenever the least opportunity offers, even though that means hauling the sledge over long stretches of shore blown clear of snow by the wind. There though, if you are lucky, you can find the one thing which can lend a momentary air of festivity to sledging along the coast of Alaska: driftwood.

This you collect towards evening in great stacks; with a great deal of difficulty you can induce it to catch, and then it flares and shines and warms you in the black cold night.

It sounds so lovely, a warming, flaming camp-fire in the raven black night of the high arctic latitudes. And it is lovely, but only for a while, for the heat of it scorches your skins and almost roasts one side of your body, while the frost jabs its icy darts into the other. If there is no wind, it is possible to achieve a feeling of real warm comfort even in biting cold by lighting two fires fairly close together and sitting between them. If you do that, however, you must beware of letting tiredness and the warmth make you drowsy and perhaps fall asleep, for the least breath of air will send the flames fanning this way and that—which can be very dangerous indeed for a man who is dozing and may easily cost a sleeping person his life. Thus, it is wisest, if less pleasant, to roast on the one side nearest to the fire and let yourself be frozen to the marrow on the other. That way, at least, your mind is at rest, and then it is always possible to turn yourself round so that heat and cold alternate.

It may sound a bit tedious, but it can be fun when conditions are good to sit by a flaming and gaily crackling camp-fire and cook the dogs' supper in a large petrol tin. A multitude of enormous stars twinkle and sparkle in the black vault that also serves as backcloth for the Northern Lights which sweep across the heavens like airy faintly coloured draperies. In a ring round the fire sit your hungry dogs, eyes sparkling in the glare of the flames, tongues long and drooping, teeth gleaming white in the firelight, giving vent to little yawns of expectation, for they know that in a short while they are going to be served the most heavenly feed.

But even they must suffer disappointment before they can attain the highlight of their day, for the boiled dog food has to be cooled a bit before it can be given to such voracious creatures, and they squeal with disappointment when the hot and delicious-smelling food is borne off into the tent and put under guard while it cools. You can so well understand their bitter disappointment. They are always starvingly hungry, and that thick gruel of rye flour, some-times with a piece of meat or two added, perhaps too a little fish or whatever you have been able to get hold of on that coast where you don't worry too much whether or not food is quite fresh, does not taste at all bad. I know that from personal experience, for I often had to share the dogs' hot dinner, because my own provisions were all used up. I won't say that it always smelt so very nice, but if you were hungry, it went down all right.

It is a joy to see the eagerness with which the dogs gulp down their food when it has cooled sufficiently not to harm them. Hurry, of course, is a necessity, for bitter experience will have taught them that the comparatively hot food in some mysterious way vanishes into the snow right under their very noses and is gone, however much they dig and scrape. Their own portion having been eaten, or having vanished, they lick their chops and sniff around in case they may find a bit which has been overlooked.

If I should have forgotten to remove the tin in which I had cooked their food, some particularly pushful dog might try to sneak an extra helping by licking the inside, where bits might con-ceivably have been left behind. There was never much to be got, and the punishment for gluttony was immediate, painful and noisy, one which could be heard for miles around and was long remembered, for, the frost being very hard, the thin tin would have already acquired roughly the temperature of the air, which would be 50° F below freezing and often more, so that the moment the dog began to lick at the bottom of the tin its damp tongue would freeze fast to it. That was a horrible thing, for with its head caught inside the tin, the poor dog would stagger about blindly, howling pitiably with the pain of it, colliding with every stone or unevenness in the ground as it fled blindly from the noisy incomprehensible torment which kept pace with it however far or fast it ran.

When that happened, you had to catch the dog, for otherwise it might go right off in its senseless fear and die, or else its tongue would get frost-bitten and it would have to be shot. It could be difficult enough to get hold of such a terrified, suffering animal and then haul it into the tent, where you cautiously applied warmth to the frozen tin and so released the dog's tongue, which for days would bear an open, smarting wound. Yet even though that painful experience was long remembered, it could be forgotten, and one evening when the dog was particularly hungry and the opportunity presented itself, the same thing could happen all over again.

Quite a number of Eskimoes lived along the coast, and every now and again things panned out well and, after many hours of sledging in the cold and dark, we would come to a little settlement and be able with a good conscience to accept a friendly Eskimo's invitation to spend the night with him.

It wasn't easy to bring oneself to refuse such invitations: the warmth of the hut was a great inducement, and so was the food for both man and dogs, which we knew would be produced in a short while, and might already be ready. And not the least of the attractions was the fact of being able to stretch out on the warm bunk together with other people, be warmed by them and hear the news of the few things which happened on the Alaskan coast in wintertime. Of course, what one wanted to know most of all was that constant concern of the sledger: what is the going like further on? What wind and weather do those with local knowledge expect for the morrow?

Thus there was good reason to stay with the hospitable Eskimoes, and as a rule I did so. But—yes, there was a 'but' connected with their hospitality and the duties and rights of host and guest it entailed. I put my foot into it once or twice, sinning grievously against the unwritten laws of hospitality, and thus I learned to be cautious, and, before I said yes or no, I would try to discover whether the master of the house had abandoned the ways of his ancestors and the age-old Eskimo customs, or whether he was one of the not inconsiderable number on the north coast in 1907 who still clung to the ways and customs which their fathers had held inviolable, a sacred inheritance from a dim and distant past.

If I got the impression that the people in that hut and in the settlement generally had had sufficient dealings with the white man not to hold too strictly to the old ways, then I gladly accepted their invitation and looked forward to a peaceful night under such good conditions that only lice might worry me a little. It was also a very great relief not to have to fumble with stiff-frozen fingers disentangling the dogs' harness, not to have to pitch the tent, make a fire, and cook food, for all those jobs were gladly done by the natives as a not unimportant part of a host's duties.

The moment I accepted an invitation to spend the night in one of those huts on the coast, my day's labours were over, and I could with a good conscience crawl into the warm hut with its smiling, chattering women, who were always so delighted with even the shortest break in the monotony of the long night of winter which the arrival of a guest meant, and which also gave them what was of inestimable value in their solitude, something fresh to talk about. Whether it were true or not, did not matter greatly, merely that it should be new and exciting.

They chattered and laughed, the merry women, and made themselves very busy getting food ready and doing other of the women's jobs. The little space soon became filled with steam and the fumes of greasy food, mixed with all the indefinable acrid smells of many and not too cleanly bodies which were an almost tangible constituent of every Eskimo hut on the coast of Alaska.

When the men and the bigger boys had unloaded the sledge and put your things safely out of reach of greedy animals, fed your dogs and all the rest of it, they would come and join the family circle, into the warmth, the stench and the untidiness of the hut, as delighted as the women, asking your news and telling you theirs. They would probably moan a bit about bad hunting, but as they did so, they would be reaching out for large lumps of steaming meat, stuffing it into their mouths and cutting off what they could not get in just in front of their lips to wait for the next mouthful, dipping their fingers into whale-oil and licking them clean with great gusto. What with the heat in the hut and the mighty meal they ate they would begin to perspire, and the sweat would pour down their faces and bodies, and they would belch and make other explosive noises which are seldom heard at table outside of primitive societies.

It was really most pleasant to be a guest in an Eskimo hut which was well supplied with meat, especially when a storm was sweeping across that desolate country, driving clouds of snow and powdered ice, laying hold of the huts and making them rock in its grasp for all their stout and stiff-frozen turf walls.

By the next day when you had to go on, or when there came a pause between the storms, your furs would have been dried and mended, your *kamiks* gone over and put right, or perhaps replaced by new ones if the old had been too hopelessly worn; the dogs' traces would have been repaired or renewed, all your harness would be like new—it was lovely.

It was, indeed, a relief for tired and hungry sledgers to be able to spend the night in such a hut, to meet people who gladly gave of the little they had, who tried to persuade you to stay longer with them and who came with you to help for quite a distance when you set out again. But you could also hit upon a hut whose occupants still clung to the age-old ways they had inherited from their ancestors, which were quite foreign to the white man's idea of the duties of a guest and which could give rise to considerable difficulties and cause discord to take the place of the hospitable helpfulness, which to the Eskimo was the first duty of a host and had been from long before the white man came to the country.

In those huts the women would also be busied preparing food, dragging the furs off the stranger so that they could be dried, chewed and kneaded till they became as soft and supple as the finest cloth, or repaired where they were torn or worn.

In those huts too the atmosphere would be festive, when a stranger sought shelter there from storm or darkness; there was the same chattering and babbling, the same merry eyes and smiling mouths; there too you felt yourself to be really welcome and looked forward to a warm sleep when the work was done—looked forward

to lying on the sleeping-platform together with the many inhabitants of the hut, to feeling the warmth of those sleeping bodies
and hearing their quiet breathing.

The first time I spent a night with Eskimoes who stuck to their
time-honoured conception of hospitality, it did not turn out as
well as I had hoped, and I failed miserably in my duties as a guest.
When, after a lot of hard eating, I followed the example of the
others and crawled on to the platform to sleep, I squeezed up close
to a giggling young beauty so as to leave room between me and
the master of the house for the latter's wife who was then sitting
on the floor in front of the oil lamp mending my skins and trousers.

She was no beauty, that Eskimo wife. Her face was as flat as
though it had been sat on when it was still new and soft and cap-
able of being moulded; it was, too, wrinkled and furrowed, ravaged by the biting snows of many winters and the burning suns of
as many summers, and her naked body was obese and bulgy, and
down it ran a number of little rivulets of sweat.

But she was industrious and she could sew, also she could chew
away at the skin-side of furs and trousers without risk of biting
holes in them, for her teeth were worn to the gums with all the
skins she had chewed in a long and hard-working life.

I lay on the bunk like all the others, watching the woman at her
work and rejoicing at the thought that in the morning I would put
on clothes which were whole and soft, admiring her skill in using
needle and thread, which was none of the modern stuff which
goes to pieces at the first stress, but caribou sinews which she had
twisted into threads, first chewing them soft in her mouth and then
rolling them smooth and even on her greasy, sweaty cheek.

I lay there comfortably, enjoying life and the respite from my
labours. The only thing I didn't like, one that was not too promising for a quiet night, was the empty place between the master of
the hut and myself. That allowed a lot of cold air in between the
two of us, so for the time being I tried spreading myself out as
much as I could between my host and the smiling girl, so that all
three could benefit from each other's warmth, but my host only

edged further away and, however much I spread myself, there was always room for one between him and me.

At last the old woman had finished with my skins and came waddling towards the platform, crawled on to it and filled the empty space—while her husband nodded to me and said hospitably: 'She has been a long time mending your things, but she's finished now and you needn't freeze any longer—she's yours as long as you stay with us!'

I tried to explain that the white man's customs were quite different, and that sort of thing wasn't even right for the Eskimoes. But he insisted and hospitably and gaily shoved her across to me, an utterly apathetic body which to look at and feel was more like a misshapen sack of wool, then he turned over on his side and prepared to go to sleep.

By now I had realized that by refusing his wife I was infringing one of the duties of a guest which had its roots in the remote past, and I hated the idea of wounding the good man who had received me so hospitably and done everything he could to make me feel at home with him. I made another attempt to explain and mitigate my refusal to pursue my rights as a guest to the absolute limit, but it was no use. Angry wrinkles furrowed my host's face, and he made me feel ashamed by saying: 'She has given you food, she has mended your skins and done them well, and I give her to you for the night, the woman who for many years has shared good times and bad with me. What more do you want?'

The atmosphere in the hut was becoming somewhat charged and intolerable: the angry husband, the obese sweaty lump between us, and then the giggling girl on my other side. If it had been she who was being offered on the altar of hospitality, we should have had little to quarrel about. But no, the custom was that the guest should have the host's wife whatever she was like, and the end of this excess of hospitality was that I got off the platform, put on my clothes and seated myself in a corner of the hut, while the dozen grown-ups there glared at me bright-eyed in profoundest disapproval of my queer behaviour and wonderment at this extra-ordinary stranger who had come to their house.

The young girl's giggles, however, turned into squeaky laughter, and she gave me a roguish, alluring look. It was neither very easy nor edifying to act chaste Joseph in the land of the Egyptians.

That was a cold and nasty night. My whole body was stiff and sore by the time it had turned into dark day and we were able to get up and make ready to leave—without help of any kind and without the warm meal we had hoped to get before we went on again on our way towards Point Barrow.

CHAPTER XII

CONFLICT BETWEEN OLD AND NEW

*Point Barrow in the wintertime—The sun goes into winter quarters—
I sledge on alone southwards—Solitary white people on the coast—The
hospitality of the Eskimoes decreases with the latitude—Hope of an
Eskimo Jesus—Rigorous sledging in cold and storm—Eskimoes make hard
business men—An emergency dwelling—The hardest stage—Point Hope*

AFTER a trip lasting two or three weeks we sledged into Point
Barrow along a hard-trodden track together with a number of
Eskimoes, all in their finery, going to the church whose tiny bell
was pealing to summon the native congregation to God's house.
The Reverend Dr Spriggs, missionary, physician and schoolmaster,
healer of bodies and souls, builder of a new age, expounded the
day's text to the listening Eskimoes. At first they were devout
enough, though eyes and thoughts were inclined to stray, but then
Dr Spriggs said something to the effect that God looked with anger
upon the woman who went up the mountain with a man she had
not taken in matrimony, and on the man who usurped the husband's place in another man's house.

The Point Barrow Eskimoes could not listen to that, nor understand it, either, for all the white men at that big settlement, naturally with the exception of Dr Spriggs, went openly and joyfully up
the mountainside with the pretty girls, and were often to be found
in houses where they had no real business to take them. In Point
Barrow, as in so many other places, theory and practice were
pretty distinct.

My few dogs were incapable of going further by the time I
reached Point Barrow, but I was given others by Mr Brower, the
local big whaling man, big trader and everything else that can be
big in an Eskimo settlement—also a big womanizer and supporter
of a tremendous pack of children. And from Brower I also got provisions for my further journey, both of us discreetly saying nothing

123

about payment. He, of course, had much more than he could use, and I nothing, and then it is the unwritten law of the wilds that he who has gives to him who hasn't.

There at Point Barrow I parted company with Axel Andersen, and although I knew that from then on I should be alone, or at best in the company of chance Eskimoes who happened to be going my way, I liked the idea and was glad. I was even more glad that Axel and I had not gone on to the pack-ice alone together, for though he was nice enough and strong enough, he could not have stood up either physically or morally to the hardships of the ice.

So, after all, it was as well things had gone as they had.

I had to hurry on. The winter was becoming more severe, not that it wasn't severe enough already. Storms swept across sea and land, driving the snow in great clouds ahead of them, and the sun went into hibernation while I was at Point Barrow. From then on sledging was not going to be easy.

It was, however getting near the full moon and that would help a bit, thus there was no time to lose, and so, with my team of fresh strong dogs and my sledge well loaded with provisions, I thanked John Brower for his help and drove off southwards. I kept urging on the dogs, in the vain hope of being able to make such swift progress to the south that I should soon once more be able to see the sun gliding along the southern horizon at midday like reddish-golden fire.

But I did not achieve that for some time. Slowly as the sun moved southwards, my progress was even slower, and it was not till the sun had reached the southern tropic and was on its way back to meet me that I saw the longed-for sight of it—but by then Christmas was over and half of January gone.

Alone I struggled along the land as best I could, in storm or calm, with the wind against me or behind, as it happened to be. The gleam of daylight at noon grew fainter and fainter every day, but, as long as the moon was in the sky and more or less full, its cold beams gave me light, as did the Northern Lights when they flared across the black vault of the sky and all but eclipsed its carpet of twinkling stars.

Occasionally I fell in with other sledgers on their travels. On-comers were no use to me, though I would stop them to ask what the going was like farther on; but if they were going in my direction I greeted them joyfully, as long as their pace was such that we could keep company.

Now and again the dogs scented people and led me either to solitary huts in the wilds, or even quite considerable settlements with an American schoolmaster or schoolmistress, and how delighted they would be to have a sort of fellow-countryman come sledging up at a time of the winter when all sensible people normally stayed indoors. It was a real joy to be with these solitary white men, to see their delight at your unexpected visit, to eat well of their good food, to talk half the night of everything under heaven not least of their work and its results. And how good it was to to be able to sleep on the floor in a room where you could breathe freely without filling your lungs with all sorts of evil exhalations —and go on again the following morning accompanied for quite a distance by the teacher who would give his children the day off to enable him to spend longer with that welcome rarity, a visitor.

Sometimes, a storm would be scouring the land and ice when I reached such a house, and then I would make myself comfortable for a day or two till the weather improved, have a good wash, and for a short while feel like a civilized person again.

But it could also happen that, at that time of the day called evening in lands where day and night alternate as they should, I would come to an Eskimo hut where I hoped for a hospitable reception, though I would be by no means sure of one, for as I gradually came further and further south of Point Barrow to regions where the influence of the white man had been felt for decades, the Eskimoes became less hospitable and more calculating.

They had of course learned quite a lot from the white men, had certainly also suffered bitter disappointments at their hands, and their pleasure in receiving an unexpected visit from one was usually directly proportional to the weight of his provisions-box—or the number of bottles he had! They turned out willingly enough and helped the tired traveller to unload his sledge and see to his dogs, but they were the whole time on the look-out for his provisions-box and assessing its possibilities.

East of Point Barrow the Eskimoes still observed the traditional custom of giving the stranger such food as they had in their houses, whether it was good or poor, plentiful or meagre, they would share even their last scrap without complaint with one who had less than they. But south of Point Barrow your Eskimo hosts regarded it as their incontestable right to have some of their visitor's provisions if he wanted to spend the night with them, or even just to rest for a while in shelter and warmth and have some warm food before he went on. That attitude became more and more prominent the farther south I went along the coast to where the Eskimoes had had considerable dealings with white people.

Thus you had to keep a good eye on your provisions-box and its contents when spending the night in an Eskimo hut, and if after a long day's sledging the warmth and fug of the hut got the better of you, and you fell asleep before the meal was cooked and eaten, you usually had to suffer for it in the days to come.

I learned that with a vengeance at Icy Cape, or was it perhaps at Wainwright Inlet, whose inhabitants did not have the best reputation on the coast? There had been a storm raging all day, and I was more than tired when I blew into the settlement. I flung myself down in the first hut I came to and fell asleep without having time to issue the day's food ration. I slept the sleep of the just, slept and slept until I awoke half-suffocated by heat and cooking fumes to see two sweating Eskimo women bent over a red-hot stove busily making large pancakes with my flour and frying thick slices of my bacon.

I rubbed my eyes in horror and yelped in dismay, for there piled on a plank were twenty-seven thick pancakes, looking tempting enough even though they were dripping with whale-oil. Beside them was another pile of singed slices of bacon, a whole seven pounds of it, all I had, the treat I had been reserving for special occasions. My flour was all gone, used to the last scraping, and all my tea had found its way into their pot, and tea is far better than coffee for keeping body and soul together on icy days of sledging.

It was no wonder the vapours of cooking had woken me out of even that deep sleep, but unfortunately it was too late. I ate pancakes and bacon till I was gasping, but I could not manage it all—which, too, I was not intended to do, it being the nice easy custom on that part of the coast that the inhabitants of a hut regarded any left-overs from the meal cooked for a visiting traveller as their rightful share, the crumbs from the rich man's table.

That feast cost me dear later on, however, and it was a long time before I forgot the grasping Eskimoes of that coast.

Hospitality was not the only thing in which you noticed an abrupt change in the Eskimo character when you got beyond Point Barrow. The balance in the pagan, independent Eskimoes' way of life which was the natural result of thousands of years of hard living in relatively straitened circumstances and in complete isolation from the outside world, had been thoroughly upset by the white man's interference with their customs, the enlightenment thrust upon them by the schoolteachers and by the missionaries' well-intentioned efforts to convert the heathen Eskimo to the Christian faith. But unfortunately, at the same time as ready hospitality disappeared and cupidity took its place, there emerged— what can one call it? not Christianity as we have understood it, but an intermediary stage between paganism and real religion, which the Christian Alaskan Eskimoes thought must be pleasing to the white man's God, from what they had heard from the missionaries on the coast.

I came to one hut south of Wainwright Inlet whose occupants called themselves Christians and had a prayer for everything or prayed over everything: they mumbled a prayer of thanks to God for my arrival, prayed over the food that was to be cooked, over the pot and its contents, prayed when the food was ready and we were about to eat, thanked God for what I had eaten, and for what they got. And when I was presumptuous enough to want to wash, the whole lot prayed in chorus over the water—presumably to avert harm from any evil spirits there might be in it and which perhaps might be contemplating drowning me or doing something to hurt me. Water was obviously a pretty dangerous thing to come in contact with on that part of the coast.

The Eskimoes in that hut were able to speak English, as could almost all on the more southerly stretch of the coast, and they showed off by praying both in English and in their own tongue. It was an orgy of prayer, but when they considered that God had been given what could reasonably be considered his due, they turned to something else they had learned from the white man, though it had little to do with Christianity: cards! But they didn't begin till they had prayed long and fervently for luck.

And how they played! It was a sort of poker, and the stakes were high. I remember one night hearing a man gamble away all his clothes, his sledge, his dogs, his rifle—and his wife. Then, as he thought I was asleep and wouldn't hear what was going on around me, he next staked what he hoped to be able to steal from my sledge before I went on. He lost even that, but I took good care to see that the winner didn't get his winnings.

I must admit, however, that the Eskimoes in that hut were the worst I met, whether for praying or gambling. But then I imagine they must have thought themselves in league with the Almighty, for I heard later that when one of the young girls in the hut became pregnant—a not unusual thing to happen on the coast—they started a rumour a few months afterwards which spread far and wide that the child she carried in her womb was an Eskimo Jesus.

That caught on with those credulous people, and from south and north the Eskimoes flocked to that lonely hut with the pregnant maiden, bringing quantities of meat and blubber, as offerings, as well as fine skins, dogs and sledges, the best that they had—for they wanted to be sure of a place in the Eskimo paradise.

When the pains began there was an expectant but miserably

Eskimo woman dancing to a drum.

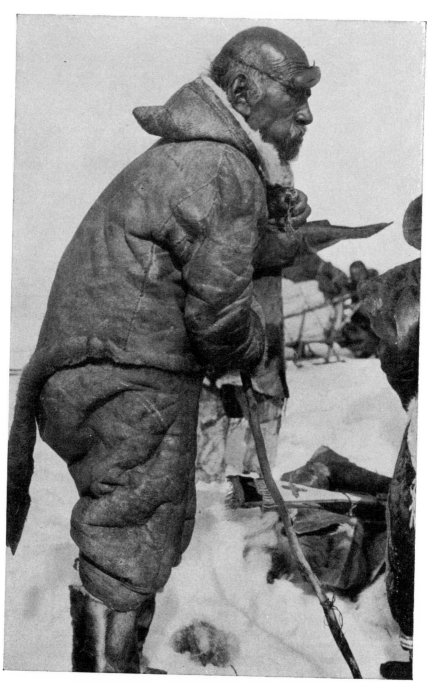

Old Eskimo.

cold multitude outside the hut, and I can imagine that they prayed so that you could have heard the noise of it for miles around. But the expectant rejoicing at the good fortune which was about to befall the Eskimo people, turned abruptly to wrath when the child was born and proved to be—a girl!

It was no use trying to explain that an Eskimo Jesus could just as well be a woman, for the Eskimoes had no great respect for women in those unenlightened days; thus great was the grief in the hut when the result was known, for though the girl and her enterprising family had for some considerable time lived well on the offerings of meat and blubber, there still remained the skins, the dogs, the sledges and all the more imperishable things. These the embittered angry Eskimoes took with them, and also anything else in the hut they could lay their hands on, and went to their homes, deeply shocked and horrified at some people's craftiness. They shunned the hut, cursed it and all it contained, just as I had done, when sledging became possible again, for I took with me from the hut many more living creatures than I had when I came to it, a whole host of them, and the crawling and itching in my hair and on my body for a long time kept alive the memory of that hut south of Wainwright Inlet.

There followed a succession of bad days with storm and swirling snow, piercing cold, appallingly bad and heavy going across wind-swept sandy beaches or high heaped sea-ice with soft snow between its sharp-edged blocks.

We toiled and laboured, the dogs and I, yet our progress was slow, for the dogs' paws were cut to pieces by the heavy hauling across the sharp gravel and stones on the wind-swept beach. I had only very little food for the poor brutes who were as hungry as I, and a couple of the weakest died and were used to feed the others.

If I was to accomplish my journey and get to milder climes I would have to have more dogs. The Eskimoes on that part of the coast proved to have been apt pupils of the whites, and they exploited the situation for all it was worth. They realized that I had to have dogs, and I remember haggling throughout one whole night over one dog. I got it in the end, but when I sledged away it was without my rifle, though I comforted myself with the thought that now I didn't have that to lug about, it was nevertheless a very unsafe feeling to be all by yourself in that wilderness with no other weapon than a sheath-knife. I might always meet a hungry bear which had scented something edible, and it would not be easy to come off best from such an encounter without a rifle.

Those, however, were just empty fears conjured up by the solitude and desolation around me, for so far I had never seen a bear on that coast, and I never met one afterwards. But when you travel alone through the wilds your senses are tensed to the utmost. Many are the weird sounds you hear: cries and whimpers, shrieks and heavy footfalls—and all behind your back. And even though you know that it is only the ice being tortured in the iron grip of the frost, the uncanny sounds will often make a solitary, tired man imagine that a bear is following his tracks, or that evil beings are stealing up behind and glaring at him with ferocious eyes. That can be unpleasant enough, especially in the dark or in thick snow—and all the more so when you have been compelled to sell your rifle and have nothing left with which to defend yourself against all the things which conceivably could be abroad in the night. And they are not few, once your imagination has taken fright.

As a rule I had an icy headwind to contend with, not so seldom half a gale and now and again a full gale, yet once or twice the clerk of the weather arranged for a following breeze, and then I rigged up a pair of skis on the sledge as a mast and set the tent or whatever else would catch the wind as a sail, and off we went across stone and ice so fast that the sledge complained and writhed as though in pain. At first the dogs could not believe that the powers above were helping them on their laborious way, but before long they were streaking ahead for all they were worth, their tails came up and waved like little banners, and they looked at me and gave delighted little whimpers.

Such sledging was a real joy, as long as you did not have to do it on an empty stomach. Despite all the things against us, we made such good progress southwards that one day I saw the upper edge of the sun peep above the low coast in the south. That was an occasion for rejoicing, and I hoped then that luck would be with me after that, and that I would see a little more of the sun every day, until the whole glorious disc showed above the horizon in all its reddish-golden splendour. But the next day the wind was against me once more and the sun hidden by clouds and drifting snow. And, what was worst of all, I blindly drove the sledge on to a stone and smashed it: one runner was broken beyond all possible repair; my progress was halted. The only good thing was that almost at the same time the dogs scented a house, and by following the scent took me to a little hut where I told my troubles to some thoroughly unsympathetic Eskimoes who had seen that my provision-box was empty.

'We can sell you a sledge,' they told me, when they had brought the wreckage and my few things into the house. 'But it is dear,' they added having cast an appraising glance at what was left of the old. All night we haggled about the miserable sledge they offered me. I had to have it; but I had no money and only a few pieces of equipment which I laid one by one on the floor, a little heap of odds and ends worth very little, yet of inestimable value to me. Still, the Eskimoes shook their heads; they wanted more, and in the end I threw down on top of the heap the last thing I had of any value, my compass, my pathfinder in darkness and blizzard.

So I got the sledge, and into the bargain a little half-spoiled meat for my dogs and myself, and the next morning I went on southwards with little but my sleeping-bag and my patched tent— I had managed to retain them—and all my papers and diaries which were of no value to the Eskimoes.

I felt bitter and remembered all the things I had given the Eskimoes in the day of my plenty; but the going was appalling and the toil and difficulties of sledging soon drove all thoughts from my head but that of getting on despite the adverse conditions, for that was the only thing which really mattered now.

For a couple of days I managed pretty well with the rotten meat, which wasn't so bad as long as it was frozen, but which was vile as soon as it had thawed out in your stomach. Food, however, we had to have, so, when the bad meat was all eaten, I had to kill one of the dogs, sharing its meagre flesh fairly with the others, but by then I had come so near the boundary between being and not being that I had either to get very soon to people who would share what they had with the poorest man on the coast, or else perish of hunger and exhaustion in the wilds.

Luckily the weather remained good, or rather I got a following wind, a storm from the north. Through the swirling snow I caught a glimpse of the high black cliffs of Cape Lisburne, the only bit of mountainous country on that coast, and stumbled in the dark upon a little settlement whose inhabitants seemed to be in almost as bad a plight as I, though willing enough to help until they discovered that I hadn't anything edible with me. Then their ardour cooled considerably.

However, they did have in the hut a few handfuls of flour and a small quantity of salmon which they had put aside as dog food when things had been better. Starving people are not squeamish, and when the salmon was swallowed frozen as it was, it didn't smell too badly.

A wild storm raged for two or three days, and when there was still no sign of a break, I decided to wait no longer but to defy the storm and press on, despite the local advice that I could not possibly get round Cape Lisburne till the weather improved. I felt that I had to try to get past that mighty rocky spur, so off I set and sought the shelter close under the perpendicular cliff-walls, where I could hear the storm raging high above my head.

Once, when I had to pass a ravine in the mountain wall, I felt the full force of the hurricane-like gusts, and it nearly cost me my life. The storm was tearing large stones off the top and sending them tumbling with a great din and commotion down the cliff face, sweeping others with them and starting dangerous land-slides. Then a particularly furious gust laid hold of the sledge and sent it slithering sideways, taking me and the dogs with it despite our united efforts to dig our feet in away from the land and out towards the open sea, which was boiling beneath the violent lashing of the storm only a hundred yards or so away.

An upright piece of ice saved me from being swept right in, but in colliding with it, the sledge was smashed and most of my few possessions went out to sea.

I cut through the traces to free the dogs and crawled back towards the land. Then I got on to some more or less safe ice and with stones hailing round me, some as big as I, I made my way back to the house I had insisted on leaving. My furs were torn to shreds by the sharp ice and I was frozen to the marrow by the piercing cold, when for the second time I stumbled into the little hut, whose Eskimoes now regarded me as one of themselves in distress.

They were magnificent then, those poor starving Eskimoes of Cape Lisburne. The men at once sallied out to try and find the dogs, if any were left alive, and perhaps some of my possessions. The women vied with each other in getting the stiff, frozen furs dragged off my body, cutting them where that was necessary, and rubbing life into my numbed hands, while a little old woman squatted patiently in front of me with my icy feet tucked up under her tunic and resting on her warm stomach.

My fingers and toes smarted and ached and throbbed, when the blood began to circulate again. It was almost intolerable; I writhed with pain and only wished they would leave me alone. My hands and feet, I thought, could very well thaw out on their own, slowly and less painfully. But the Eskimoes knew what was at stake, and despite my protests they went on patiently thawing my hands and feet until I collapsed, exhausted. And some hours later, when the men returned with three of my dogs and the sack with my papers, diaries and such, the women had to start all over again on them, for they were frozen and their furs torn.

The storm raged on for a couple of days yet, and when it eventually subsided slightly, I made another attempt to get away, but had to give up once again. The open water now extended right up to the land and breakers were spurting high up the perpendicular cliffs which were sheathed in ice and hung with long icicles; it was gloriously beautiful; but the intervals between the ice-floes in the sea were too great for me to be able to jump from one to the other.

It was bitter having to go back to the hut yet once again, to the grinning yet sympathetic Eskimoes who had warned me not to attempt the impossible. It was hard to go back to eating half-rotten fish without even a mug of tea to wash your throat clean with after it. Life was grim.

We were all in a pretty desperate plight, yet the Eskimoes laughed at me, the silly white man, who got annoyed unnecessarily at what could not be changed. It doesn't help in the least, they told me, the storm will stop sometime; no one has ever heard of a storm which lasted all winter. Take things calmly. We'll share with you the little food we have; you won't be any worse off than we. And when the storm abates, then you can go. It isn't so far to Point Hope, to other white men who are just as absurd as you and rush off after—yes, after what?

They could not think what it was, those natural philosophers, who took life and the dispensations of providence as they came, with never a murmur. Man could not alter things in any way. And they questioned me closely in an attempt to discover why I was in such a hurry that I was prepared to hazard my life to get away and had already done so twice. They discussed it among themselves, and eventually thought they had found the explanation: somewhere far from Cape Lisburne there must be a white girl to whom my thoughts kept going. They could not think of any other reason for my foolishness. And they laughed at my protests, did not believe me—there were girls enough there in the hut, one old wrinkled man told me, take one of them as the other white men are accustomed to do, take two if you want. Relax for a bit, the weather will turn good again sometime.

And it did. On the ninth day after my first arrival at the hut the wind abated sufficiently for there to be reasonable hope of being able to get past that thrice-accursed Cape Lisburne. Others of the occupants of the hut were also starved out, so it was quite a little caravan which moved off towards the rocky promontory. Most of them, however, turned back when they saw the waves of the open sea breaking against the ice-clad base of the rock. However, by jumping from one ice-floe to the next, as they swirled about in the grip of the currents and winds, I eventually got round the cape and reached Point Hope after some thirty hours of hard going, carrying my few possessions in a sack fastened on my back and followed by my three dogs.

CHAPTER XIII

THE WORST IS OVER

A meeting with acquaintances—Fresh sledging equipment—A man on his way home—To town for Christmas—A merry host—A Christmas murder—A suspicious telegraph operator—Fresh equipment again—The sun emerges from its winter quarters—Death comes to Death Valley

I T was lovely to be in a house again, a proper house, and to sit at a table and eat, be able to eat without wondering whether there would be enough for the morrow. They were a decent lot, those men in that northern outpost; they couldn't do enough for me.

They marvelled that I had been able to get through all the way from Flaxman Island, alone and in the darkness of the winter night, and they refrained from mentioning my ship which had lain at anchor there the year before, filled with equipment and provisions and the flag of hope fluttering aloft. They kept their questions about the undiscovered land, until I myself thought it proper to speak of it and told them that I had not found land, but that I still believed in its existence.

They gave me some dogs, which was all the more precious a gift as they were not rich men giving of their abundance; and they gave me a sledge to take the place of the two I had smashed on the way, and also provisions, and that made it possible for me to sledge on whenever it suited me. And their plump Eskimo women sewed me a new set of furs in place of the patched tatters in which I had arrived.

Those were happy days I spent at Point Hope. The settlement's father, Rev. Dr Driggs, missionary and schoolmaster, and even qualified physician, showed the way, and the others all vied to make life easy for me while I was their guest, and to give what help they could for what lay ahead: the long distance I still had to cover before I reached Nome. Those were men who themselves had struggled and toiled, and who knew from bitter experience that tomorrow they might well be in the same straits as I was then.

They were fine those white men at Point Hope, magnificent to me in my distress—and I wondered whether I had not perhaps judged the whites on that coast too hardly.

Most of the Eskimoes there spoke English, as, indeed, they had all along the coast from Point Barrow; some so that you could understand them more or less, others very well. That was not only the result of Dr Driggs' teaching, however, for several of the men and older youths only lived there in winter-time, going south to Candle City when the sun returned and the ice melted on sea and land, to work for the white gold-diggers there. They were well enough paid for their work, and their houses were full of the weirdest assortment of useless things bought with the money they had earned. Money they had no understanding of, and they thought they had done a magnificent stroke of business if they were given a dollar piece or two for a seal for which they had cheerfully asked ten dollars.

From Point Hope I had the company of a trader who wanted to buy some tins of baking powder in Candle City. When I left, it was with dogs which were comparatively fresh and a better sledge than I had had for a long time. We sledged across the ice or land, whichever suited best, but mostly on land, as the many storms had blown the ice far out to sea in Kotzebue Sound, and there was none at all to be seen from Jabbertown.

In a violent snowstorm in which we lost all sense of direction and had to leave it to the dogs to find the way, we came to a little cluster of houses, a very small town called Blossom, though I doubt if there could have been one flowering plant to be found on that wind-swept shore even in the height of summer. The name, I suppose, was the result of man's desire to remember the beauties of his home, while out there in the wilds where you freeze to the marrow, and drifting snow makes heavens and earth merge into one.

Anyway, that little place was called Blossom, and no doubt it will continue to be so as long as its houses stand. It was there that I met a fellow countryman, who introduced himself as Hans Holm from the island of Bornholm. He was trader, whaler, owner and skipper of a schooner with an Eskimo crew, magistrate and official Registrar of Claims in a district where no gold had yet been found, but where Holm felt certain that he would find his bonanza sooner or later. And it would be a rich find, when he made it, he assured me. He was a fine, enterprising man, a super-optimist, given to dreaming splendid dreams of a not too distant future, when he would have collected enough treasure to be able to leave rich Alaska and go home to Bornholm, where he would use the gold he hoped to find in the generous lap of Blossom to buy a farm which must lie on a sunny slope covered with pretty flowers and facing south.

But I doubt if he ever went home to Bornholm, for he would certainly never be able to go back to ordered conditions of life. But he did get to Candle City, for he thought that I was sledging so badly that he must help a fellow-countryman—and perhaps too he thought it would be pleasant to celebrate Christmas with me—at any rate, at the last moment he decided to come with me, and we reached Candle City together on Christmas Eve.

That really was going to town and a great excitement for such wanderers as Holm and me. Candle was a fairly large town which had grown up like a mushroom on the rumour of gold, though not just the rumour, for there was gold there. When Holm and I came sledging up the river on Christmas Eve we saw the lights twinkling on the banks where busy, sweating men were breaking the frozen earth with pick-axes and dynamite in order to cash the golden treasure they had travelled so far to find.

They called to us, unknown wayfarers in the night, to halt and come and eat with them, they would give us bread and a juicy haunch of caribou and rum to go with it, rum which would drive all care from your mind and cold from your body. Those were kindly offers and to begin with we were easy to persuade, but gradually as our stomachs became full and the feeling of cold vanished, as we had been promised, we grew more independent, especially as, having heard in detail from the first Candle man we met how, when and why one of the city's publicans had just been shot a couple of hours earlier, we could not reward those who offered us their hospitality by listening interestedly to the same story, with whatever variations, for the umpteenth time, so we drove on adamantly and reached the city late that evening.

I had sledged the one thousand miles between Flaxmann Island and Candle City in seventy days, mostly alone, always in darkness, storm or drifting snow, exhausting a score of dogs and reducing three sledges to matchwood.

I was tired, but satisfied, as I drove up the brightly lit main street with its fine shops, and I heaved a great sigh of relief when, for the last time on that long journey, I called 'whoa' for my dogs to stop. That job was done!

The journey had taught me to be easily satisfied both as regards quarters and food, and I could not help giving a gasp of amazement when the smiling innkeeper, who had just lost a keen competitor, showed me into a room with a proper bed, more or less clean sheets, a table and a chair or two, and where not far away was a bathroom with hot water in the bath—that was real luxury, almost too much of a good thing!

Washed and combed, in as far as it had been possible to get a comb through my matted hair, comparatively free of lice and clad in the publican's best suit, I preferred to celebrate Christmas in the hotel's restaurant where the tables were covered with red-spotted cloths. There stood mine host, ready to serve: 'Friend from the wilds, what would you like to have?'

The good man reeled off all the things the house could provide and they were not few: Haunch of caribou, elk steak, boiled or grilled salmon, an orgy of food. And I sent for it all, felt as though I could never be satisfied, ate and ate, shovelling it in with both fork and knife while the man stood beside me, laughing: 'Have some more, stranger, glad to see you've an appetite, and there's more than you can eat here!' 'Splendid,' said I, when he brought me a dish of pancakes to end up with, large pancakes glistening with butter: 'Magnificent—but what will you say, innkeeper, when I tell you that I haven't a cent, not one grain of gold dust with which to pay you for this glorious meal?'

'Oh,' said he and laughed, 'I know that only too well. A hungry man straight from a long sledge journey does not think of such things—until afterwards. But, eat away; when you find gold you will give me a tenth of your claim!'

'I would gladly do so,' I told him, but added at once, 'only I have never had any gold, I have no intention of digging for gold and I never expect to get any gold. What do you say to that?'

He stood there, looking at me, then he laughed: 'Just to see you eat was well worth the money. But to meet a man up here who isn't looking for gold and doesn't think he will find gold, is so extraordinary that it must mean good fortune for me. And for that alone, you shall be my guest as long as you like. But tell me, friend,' he went on, after a little further scrutiny of me, 'there's a foreign note in your speech, you're not by any chance a Swede, are you?'

I had no idea what he was getting at, but I had eaten his food and just been invited to be his guest, thus I owed him some consideration and so I answered rather evasively: 'Not altogether that, but a Dane. It's about the same thing, we're both Scandinavians, brother peoples. But why do you ask?'

Then he told me that in the gold country the diggers were prepared to offer a lot for a Swede, or a Scandinavian, he added considerately, it would amount to the same, to be their partner, that is, someone who wasn't looking for gold and who—'Listen, friend,' the man went on, and gave me rather an anxious smile, 'you wouldn't by any chance also be innocent, would you?'

'What?' I was even more surprised. 'What do you mean?'

'Well, you see,' he said rather embarrassed, 'If you also happened never to have had anything to do with a girl and that sort of thing, then I would be dead sure to find my bonanza tomorrow or to get news that one of my partners, and I have many, had found it. But that of course is too much to hope for, that you should be innocent,' and he looked at me interrogatively, almost beseechingly.

140

'Well, perhaps it is,' said I and laughed: 'But any way let's leave it to the future to show you what sort of person it was you entertained. At least my heartiest thanks are yours for your hospitality and my best wishes for success with your diggings.'

And that was all the payment he asked or got—they were a queer lot, the people in Alaska.

That was the first time I had heard of the gold-diggers' superstition about the 'innocent' Swede, but it was by no means the last. They were strange men, those gold-diggers in Alaska: friendly, helpful and naive, yet at the same time they could also be ruthless, brutal and calculating.

A short while after that conversation with my smiling, gold-seeking host, I was able to see for myself that other side of the gold-digger's character, his boundless brutality. I was still sitting in the restaurant, in fact trying to dispose of another titbit, when a violent noisy dispute broke out among a group of men who were standing by the bar drinking neat whisky in beer glasses. They were all pretty tight, loud-mouthed and noisy, but then everyone talked big in that country, and they banged their fists resoundingly on the bar to give more weight to their loud assertions.

Two men were the centre of the altercation, but the others were noisily insistent on saying their piece, though they probably knew little—if anything—of what the quarrel was about. They quarrelled just for the sake of quarrelling, a crowd of excited men brandishing threatening fists at each other, and it was obvious that hell might break loose at any moment.

There was a hush lasting a few seconds after one of the angry men had flung at the other statements about his conduct, his mother and all his family, so insulting that it was obvious that deeds must now take place instead of words. And so they did: the next moment a fist smashed into the man's face, blood spurted from his nose and mouth.

He staggered under the violence of the blow, then as with his left hand he wiped the blood from his face, with a lightning movement of his right hand he pulled his knife from its sheath and thrust it deep into his adversary's stomach, slitting it up. The wounded man gave a yelp and collapsed. There was a deathly silence, and all you heard was the wounded man's agonized groaning, while blood gushed from his belly and spread across the floor towards me.

The killer leaned heavily on the bar and dried the bloody blade of his knife on his trousers. He was all alone now; those who a few seconds before had been vociferously backing him up had all melted away. He looked down at his fallen adversary with a hunted horrified look, then he turned to go, and the ring of men made way for him—but not so the publican, who came running up towards the bar, no longer smiling and friendly as he had been while talking with me, but with flashing eyes and his mouth a narrow slit in a pale face in which the veins stood out at his temples like quivering blue knots. He was not afraid of the man with the knife, who now flourished it threateningly, only the next moment to receive a chair on his head and to drop with a little sigh, as though he had been hit by the heavy impact of a pile-driver.

That broke the breathless tension which had reigned since the killing. Loud cries and rough oaths echoed round the room; the men gesticulated wildly and once again tried to shout each other down, but the publican told them to be quiet: 'Tie that man up before he recovers consciousness, and get the other off to the hospital; but get a move on, or it'll be too late.'

Sand was strewn on the blood-spattered floor, and ten minutes later the publican came and sat down at my table. Smiling, he nodded at the bar and the dozen or so men standing at it quietly pouring whisky down their throats: 'Yes, that's a bit different to your solitary roaming about in the darkness out there on that coast; see what it is to get back to civilization!'

Of course, you could say that I had, but in my own mind I was not altogether sure.

There was a telegraph in Candle and some rash souls lent me the money to make use of it, quite a lot of money, for telegraphing from there was expensive. However, I had to send word to Leffing-well's and my own parents contradicting the telegram from Dawson City announcing our demise in the pack-ice, so with the money in my pocket I went off cheerfully to the hut which housed the telegraph and handed in the telegrams which were to turn grief into joy in our two homes.

It didn't prove as easy as I had expected, for, when the operator had read the telegrams, he sat for a moment cogitating, then he shook his head and said: 'No, stranger it won't do. I can't accept those telegrams.'

'Why on earth not?' I was so surprised I could hardly speak, and indignation at the man's extraordinary behaviour began to bubble up inside me, but I managed to hold it in check and added: 'Naturally I have the money to pay the charge,' and I produced the bundle of borrowed dollar notes: 'Look!'

'It's not that,' replied the telegraph operator, 'but this—' and he placed a dirty finger on my name. 'Here it says that the sender is Ejnar Mikkelsen, but he died in the pack-ice last year, that was in May, I believe. The news was telegraphed from Dawson City and it was in all the papers. And now you come and want to send telegrams in his name. I can't have a hand in such a macabre jest.'

I swore at him and laughed at the same time, and slowly it dawned on the zealous man with the good memory that there might have been something funny about that telegram from Dawson City. I told him my story, and a short while later we parted more or less friends. The telegrams were sent, and the telegraph man at once shut his office, for he had to get out and tell the people of Candle City that the dead man was not dead at all, but had come to their city all the long way from Flaxman Island.

In the bustle and confusion of the previous evening I had forgotten to say where I came from, or else it had passed unnoticed in all the noise and Christmas excitement; but now the town knew, and it was made an occasion for celebration. It doesn't happen every day that someone from Flaxman Island blows into Candle City.

My dog-team had to be renewed; my sledge was no good for

land travel and I must have another, and the clothes I wore were the publican's Sunday togs, but none of that impaired our pleasure. Others had what I lacked, in fact they vied with each other to give or lend me what I needed to be able to continue on to Nome; and thus it was in splendid warm furs and driving a magnificent sledge behind a fine team of ten powerful dogs that I made my way out of Candle City, escorted by all who could tear themselves away from the city's many inns, and set off down the hard-beaten track which led across the Seward Peninsula to Nome.

All was right with my world that day and the sun contributed to my well-being by creeping out of its winter quarters after its long hibernation. Its reddish-golden rays fell on pines and fir-trees which were powdered with rime, on tall, slender-branched birches, on slope after slope which seemed to rise endlessly ahead of me, on a chalky white landscape—with very long, black shadows pointing straight towards the freezing north from which I had come.

Lovely! Magnificent! Forgotten were all the difficulties of the journey, forgotten the thrice-accursed Cape Lisburne, forgotten every piece of bad luck and adversity I had encountered, and as I drove southwards along that good track towards the resplendent sun I remembered only the fine people I had met on my journey, the pleasant hours, and even days, I had had in spite of everything.

There were other travellers than I on the track, both coming towards me and going in my direction; and as we passed we greeted each other with the joyous news all had long since seen: the sun's come back.

As I sat there on the sledge, with my companion, for I had with me another man who was also making for Nome, and drove towards that blazing conflagration in the south, snug in my warm skins, washed and clean, free of lice and other unpleasantnesses, I thought of the sun-worshippers of antiquity and understood them and their adoration of the sun, the life-giver, which rouses all living things out of their winter's torpor, draws the sprouting shoots out of black mould, places colourful flowers on green

(*Above*) Sledging along the Alaskan coast.
(*Below*) Sledging over land.

Ejnar Mikkelsen when he was the guest of Nome in the hectic days of the
Gold Rush (1907).

plants, gives a sensation of new life to both men and animals, sends the blood coursing more swiftly in their veins, and arouses the urges which create life itself.

We drove through forest where the wind was no more than a gentle soughing in the tree-tops, like a gentle fall of rime from the branches; and we drove across long stretches where the forest had been unable to take root, and where the wind howled as it had on the stern outer coast, driving snow in front of it in clouds so thick that I had to leave it to the dogs to follow the track which we could not see.

It was cold inland, and on 31 December 1907, I experienced the greatest cold I have ever sledged in or have ever measured. The mercury had long since gone stiff in its tube, but my alcohol thermometer registered 104° F below freezing! The wind, however, was with us, so that the cold was nonetheless supportable. Ahead of us the great expanse contracted and narrowed into snow-clad mountains, and all of a sudden we drove into a long, narrow valley, where the wind howled and wailed as if that were the abode of tormented souls. There the wind wrestled with the sledge and us. The place was called Death Valley and was feared by all who sledged across the Seward Peninsula.

In the middle of the valley we met three men, bent forward and struggling along against the wind and the violent drifting snow. They must have set out in a great hurry, wherever it was they had come from, for they were dressed in what sensible people would wear in a relatively warm house, but in which only mad-men would dare to go outdoors up there in the North, where you must be prepared for anything.

They had turned their jacket-collars up and were trudging northwards in ordinary leather boots, with their hands thrust deep in their trousers' pockets. They were bent forward to stem the violent gusts and the drifting snow, and when they stopped by my sledge and turned their backs to the wind to get a few moments' rest and a breather, we could see the waxen-yellow colour of death on their foreheads, cheeks, noses, chins and ears, where the rime had not even melted: they were frost-bitten everywhere where their skin was visible.

We advised them to turn back, told them they were inviting certain death if they went on walking into that biting wind, that probably they had already gone too far, but perhaps they could yet save their lives. We told them to get on to the sledge and that we would drive them as quickly as we could to a house. 'You must be crazy to want to defy such weather and cold—in that get-up,' we said.

But no, they would not listen to the well-meant advice of those who knew, for gold had been found somewhere or other in Death Valley. They had heard of it themselves from the man who had made the find and who was then in Nome registering his claim. And now they wanted to get up there and take land, before every inch was snapped up by others. Had we also staked out a claim?

All persuasion glanced off the stubborn men who had only the one thought in their heads: gold at any price. And though my companion and I debated whether to turn them back by force, we gave up the idea, as we were scarcely strong enough to overpower three desperate and inevitably armed men, who gruffly refused our offers of help and parted from us angrily and stumbled off into the swirling snow and storm, driven by those golden hopes which had failed so many, many people.

A couple of hours later we reached a hut bursting with people who were sitting round a flaming open fire, gold seekers one and all, lured there from Nome by the rumour of a find in Death Valley, yet sensible enough to remain indoors until the weather improved. We told them about the crazy, obstinate men whom we had met fighting their way against wind and cold to the north and presumably an early death, and it was agreed that some of them should go back with us along the track to overpower them and bring them to the house, if they had not . . .?

We set off again without wasting time, struggled back in that dreadful weather—and we found three bodies covered with snow, not far from where they had refused our offer of help with snarling curses. As far as we could see they were already dead, frozen to death, so we laid the bodies on a sledge and hastened back through the snow and storm. When we arrived at the hut we found that they had in fact paid the full price: life was long since extinguished.

CHAPTER XIV

IN GOLD-DIGGER COUNTRY

Nome—What a guest of the town can permit himself—An unpleasant commission—Nome's welcome gift—I am nearly drowned

THE next morning the sun was shining out of a cloudless sky; the weather was still and fine, and all the gold-seekers hurried northwards, while we continued on our way to Nome, which we reached a couple of days later, after following for some time the snowed-up little railway track, along which in the summer gold-bearing ore is brought from Salmon Creek to the 'capital of the North,' as they called Nome.

The telegraph had already announced my impending arrival, and I was met outside the town by a number of people, including the town's Scandinavians and its mayor, all freezing bravely in horse-drawn sledges decked with Danish and American flags. With chittering teeth they bade me welcome in speech and song, and the mayor mumbled something which I didn't think I had understood correctly: 'Stranger,' he said, 'welcome to Nome—as the city's guest.'

I thanked him without having any real idea what he meant, and so we drove on into the town where a great dinner was arranged for me in the 'Sons of the North' clubhouse, a festive place built of thick barked logs, its walls hung with prospectors' and hunters' trophies and with pictures of the great men of Gold-digger Land.

We ate well and drank hard; it's amazing how much you can eat and drink in the North. We feasted until I was more than satisfied, and then we went out into the streets to cool off a bit and also to see what the place looked like. It wasn't much to look at, but it was full of friendly people and smiling women, who nodded a welcome to the queer man who had sledged so far and been absurd enough to search for rumoured islands, when there was more than enough unexplored land already. Didn't the town of Nome itself lie in the middle of such country?

It was only on that walk that I fully realized the significance of the mayor's mumbled remark about being the city's guest. I was passing a public house and had either grown thirsty again or was feeling a bit chilly, for it occurred to me then that it wouldn't have been a bad thing if I had found a little gold dust, for then I should have been able to buy myself a drink to warm me up.

Someone inside must have guessed my thoughts, for out of the door came a smiling man: 'Come in, Stranger, come in and get something to drink and warm yourself.'

I did not wait to be asked twice, and received a welcome which was both noisy and wet. My glass was filled again and again; everyone seemed to want to stand a round, except me. And I wanted to, only I had no money. So I went up to the publican who looked a friendly man, said how-do-you-do and all the rest of it and eventually managed to stammer out: 'Will you give me a round on credit?'

He laughed and chuckled: 'You ask for credit! You who can buy whatever you want! I wish I was you, then you'd see!'

That was strange talk for an impecunious man to hear; I looked at him wonderingly and enquiringly, and he replied with a laugh: 'You're the city's guest, aren't you? You were told that by the Reception Committee! You can stand a round whenever you like, my friend, stand two, ten, buy the whole ruddy pub and all it contains, buy the whole darned town if you like, it's all on the town, the city pays.'

Then I realized what was what, and we had to celebrate that; we celebrated at considerable length and passers-by heard the noise and peeped in. They were all cold, all thirsty, and all had to have something to drink, all had to clink glasses with me, who was footing the bill—it was an extraordinary thing to feel like a great man and be the city's guest.

All the same, it could not go on for ever. Only half of my journey was done, and I still had a long way to travel before the open sea lay spread before my eyes, and a lot of things were to happen to me before then; so I made preparations to resume my journey and began gradually saying goodbye to the fine men I had met in Nome, hard-fisted gold-diggers, smart business men, who had all had a friendly word, though also a slightly patronizing smile, for the man who was not interested in gold.

One evening one of the biggest shopkeepers in the city came to me, talked about this and that and my long sledge trip to the open sea, things I understood and could talk about. But then he became solemn and began speaking about the crisis in America, saying how money was tight and a lot more about finance, which to my ears was just a witch doctor's gibberish of which I understood not a word.

What did financial crises and credit and all the rest of it concern me, a penniless man?

But it did all the same, for the man went on with his monologue saying something about honesty in money matters and how rare it was to find it in Nome where all had so much, but only wanted to have still more. People with gold-hunger were not ones to rely on; but a man who was not searching for gold must be differently made than others in those parts, and he had heard that I was not searching for gold, that I had no intention of looking for gold; was that true?

Yes, it was true, I told him somewhat surprised and rather embarrassed to find myself so utterly different from all the splendid chaps I had met in Nome, but whether that made me any more honest than they was not a thing on which I could express an opinion. 'Spill it out, man, what is it you want?'

And then he came out with it, the request he had been working up to with such roundabout prolixity: his associates in America would not send more goods unless he could pay a certain amount down in cash; and he had gold enough there in Nome, but no one to take it to the States—would I perhaps do that for him? It involved gold in dust and nuggets to a value of forty thousand dollars, or it may have been eighty, I have forgotten the amount, but whatever it was, it was a lot of money, enough to equip a big expedition.

I pointed out the dangers of transporting so much gold through country whose permanent or temporary inhabitants were not exactly renowned for their virtue, as he himself had said, and I told him, too, that his trust in my honesty rested on a very slender foundation, for he really didn't know that I might not be the worst of the lot and had only assumed the garb of honesty in order to exploit the credulous. To make a short story of a long night's discussion, I agreed to take his gold with me to Seattle, but I told him that I would not give him a receipt for it, and that I would hand it over to the first person who came and said threateningly: 'Out with the gold you have on your sledge, or else . . . !' I would put his bags of gold in my kitbag and let them lie there in it on the sledge, even if I was in a hut somewhere carousing with the country's most notorious highwaymen; and if a sudden thaw came, and my sledge should happen to go through the ice, I would save all my own things before I touched his damned gold. In fact, the only promise I would make which could be any sort of safeguard that his gold would reach its destination was that I would not say a word to anyone I met on my journey about having gold in my kitbag, and that I would give it to his representative in Seattle —if it ever got so far.

Those were hard conditions. He wailed and lamented, and thought that I had too little consideration for his welfare and far too little respect for gold. But he had either to be without goods in his shop that summer, or else entrust his gold to me. So, just before I left, he brought me his gold which I stuffed into my kitbag in his presence. It was hard for him to say goodbye to his lovely leather bags of gold, and he hated doing it, but then it was also hard for me to have to lug that deadweight with me all the twelve hundred long miles from Nome to the open sea. And many a time, when the going was heavy and the dogs tired, I cursed my good nature and that shopkeeper's gold, which I had let myself be persuaded to bring safely to Seattle. And about payment for my doing so, neither he nor I said a word, and that annoyed me too when my purse was empty and the prices of provisions sky-high. And it annoys me still to think that I was so stupid.

I spent the last night in Nome in the company of my friends. We celebrated until daybreak, and then I harnessed my dog-team and drove away from that hospitable town a rich man by comparison with what I had been when I arrived, because the farewell celebrations had started with a great dinner and beside my place I had found a bag of gold-dust worth five hundred dollars they told me delightedly, not so very much perhaps, but enough to cover my expenses till I got to the next big town.

That was a fine gift to receive, and they made sure that others would follow their example, for they cheerfully telegraphed to the next town: Thus and thus has Nome treated the traveller from the unknown North who seeks other things than gold. Do you do likewise! The men of Nome were not ones to hide their light under a bushel.

The example was followed, and how glad I was, for it meant that I had no acute money worries till I reached the United States and people whose attitude to money was utterly different.

I knew nothing of all that when I left Nome, however, but gradually discovered that good hospitable people in other of the little towns of Alaska had received the hint from there. And a good thing that was, for without the gold dust that was so undeservedly sprinkled over me here and there, I should have been forced to disprove the people of Nome's assertion that I was not out for gold as was everyone else in Alaska. Sledging was dear in that part of the world. A salmon for dog food, which was the cheapest thing you could get, as a rule cost three dollars each—and a bit more if the vendor discovered that your dogs were very hungry.

Experienced sledgers in Nome had advised me to cut inland at once and follow the more or less hard-trodden trail across country, but the sea had so far been my friend, and I knew what sledging along the coast involved, while inland it might produce surprises for which I was not prepared. And though the local pundits shook their heads and told me that I would bitterly rue it if I trusted to the sea-ice, I decided to follow the coast, and at first I had no reason to regret it.

But there came a day—! Well, yes, I was cheerfully sledging along by the shore, the weather was good, the sun shining with all the brightness it could muster there in the depths of winter, the going was magnificent and the sledge slipping easily along the narrow edging of ice frozen fast to the steep shore. That fringe wasn't broad, fifteen feet at the most, and where it ended was open water straight away, for the storms of the last few days had blown all the sea-ice so far out that it could scarcely be seen any longer.

The sunshine glistened on the baby wavelets which licked at the rim of the ice with a sound of chuckling which was familiar and friendly. I thoroughly enjoyed seeing all that water, where for so long I had only seen ice, and my thoughts went ahead to the day when I should again stand on a ship's deck and sail out across the sea, away from Alaska, the disappointments I had had there and also the many joys it had afforded me despite everything.

In that happy frame of mind I did not immediately notice that my dogs had begun behaving strangely, lifting their paws high and going a bit irregularly, weaving to right and left as far as the traces would let them. When I did stop to investigate, I discovered that there was water in all the little depressions in the ice. There was nothing I could do about that, so I drove on. Within a quarter of an hour, however, I realized that things had gone very wrong indeed, for the ice had suddenly become completely covered with water. I realized too late that it was about the hour of high water, and I knew that the tide there could rise quickly and very high, though I had no idea how high.

The cliff wall there was sheer and impossible to climb or even get a footing on, but round the next headland, Cape Darby, a mile and a bit away, there was supposed to be a strip of foreshore where I probably should be able to escape the swiftly rising water.

However, it was obviously going to be a race with the tide, and if it was to be won, I should have to drive the dogs harder than I liked. So I put my strength behind the long whip now dripping with water, swung it over the poor whimpering beasts and lashing them where it stung most, and myself hauled with a trace over my shoulder till the sweat was running down me, while the water from underneath seeped into my *kamiks*.

The water rose and rose above the ice; the sledge began to float, the dogs to swim in the icy water, and, to make matters even worse, darkness was beginning to fall, so that I could no longer see the ice through the water and kept falling into holes up to my waist in water. The belt of ice grew narrower and more uneven, and I splashed along through the water with deep sea a couple of yards to the right and perpendicular cliffs within arm's length on my left.

Still the water rose. I got cramp from that icy bath, and so no doubt did the dogs, which were wild with fright and pain, howling and whimpering with fear. But I kept at them with the whip; one of them drowned, had to be cut loose from the tangled traces, and so drifted out to sea.

The water was then almost up to my thighs, rising slowly but implacably. It was a question of life or death, I no longer thought of the flat foreshore a little further on; my eyes were fixed on the cliff face, surely somewhere there would be a fissure, some unevenness on which I could get a footing? At last in the dusk I saw what might be a ledge ten or twelve feet up the cliff-wall. Up we would have to get; it was our last chance.

I pulled the smallest of the dogs to me, cut its traces, threw it up the cliff wall and prayed that it would find a foothold. It did, Barking with delight at having escaped the water, it clung on, crawled up a bit further and reached the ledge, from which its glad whimpers called to the other dogs. They, encouraged by the dog on the ledge and urged to their utmost by my shouts and the whip-lash, hooked on to the little unevennesses in the rock and reached the ledge, pulling on the traces to escape the horrible water. Thus, with the dogs tugging and me pushing from behind, our united efforts eventually got the sledge safely on to land.

That ledge was only just large enough to accommodate the sledge, the dogs and me. Beneath us, the tide was rising gurgling and sucking, licking up at the cliff wall as though it were trying to sweep us back into the sea.

My clothes were sopping. There must have been 45° F of frost, and to prevent myself freezing stiff in a suit of ice-armour I had to get my dripping things off, cutting them where that would facilitate the process of changing. And change I had to, and change I did, but when groping in my kitbag for dry clothes my fingers kept finding the heavy bags of gold which had nearly drowned us all. That damned gold! How I would have loved to have chucked the muck into the sea and so rid myself of it for good; but I didn't. Was it a sort of honesty triumphing over evil instincts, or my respect for the red gold asserting iself? I certainly never thought of the shopkeeper's feelings.

I had no tent with me, for I had been told in Nome that you could drive from inn to inn, so I just had to manage without one. When the dogs had shaken the water out of their fur, and I had changed into dry things, we all huddled together as well as we could so as to keep each other warm. Above us towered the tall cliff, and higher still the host of the twinkling stars marched their way across the heavens from the east and disappeared beyond the tops of the mountains in the west, while the Northern Lights flared gaily with bunches of red, green and violet rays.

It was a long night, but the water did not get up to us, so we managed after all. When it grew light and the tide had ebbed, leaving the ice passable once more, we sledged on, and shortly afterwards reached the inn, of which I had thought all night as a paradise.

It is very seldom that reality corresponds to the Eden a hungry and exhausted man has conjured up during the long hours of a wretched night, and it did not do so here. When I reached the inn, it was vile; as dark and sour, disordered and dirty as the worst

Eskimo hut. But it could produce a flaming fire and also a little food; and since I could get from it on to the sledge-route used by the local people who were wiser than I, I there turned my back on the deceitful sea which I next saw three months later.

CHAPTER XV

THE ENDLESS TRAIL

What can happen on the sledge-trail—Its road-houses—Its grandees, women and poor devils—Rumour-mongering—Swapping tall stories— A barman's equipment and his earnings

THE much-lauded overland sledge route was supposed to be both easy to find and to follow, so those in Nome who knew had told me: 'mostly you just had to keep your eye on the telegraph line,' the thin wire of which, carried on tall poles, kept the gold district at Nome so to speak anchored to the great mother country *via* Valdez, for which I was heading. Four years before, when Nome had been the great adventure of that land of gold, they had brought those twelve hundred miles of copper wire over hill and dale, bog and river, through mighty tracts of virgin forest and across billowing plains, which a few years later were to be the home of industrious farmers, who grew corn, even wheat, where before had been a wilderness.

It sounded so easy; just 'mostly' to follow the telegraph poles through that trackless land. There couldn't surely be anything difficult in that, for the upright poles were visible for a considerable distance. Yet it wasn't so easy as I had imagined. I had in fact been surprised that those who so strongly recommended the overland sledge route had all seemed to stress the word 'mostly,' but I had attached no special significance to it. Soon I discovered, however, that it was the crux of the whole thing, for the team-drivers who had tramped the first track in the soft downy snow in the autumn, had naturally gone where the ground was best for sledging, even though that meant departing quite a distance from the telegraph line. And all the sledges which came after them had equally naturally followed their track, so as to avoid the soft snow on either side, which in midwinter lay so deep that it covered all the smaller trees with a shroud—though snow was not that, not a white shining cloth to cover up the horror of death, but a warming quilt spread by the good Lord to protect plants against the ravages of the frost and the fierce attacks of the winter storms. Thus I soon learned that, though the direction was largely given by the upright poles and the thin singing wire they carried, I had to watch for every indication of the track turning, in order to avoid myself, the dogs and the sledge sinking deep and helplessly into many feet of soft snow, as you did the moment you left the narrow track, which was not difficult to lose, as it was covered with fresh snow after every fall and every storm.

Getting back on to it was a laborious job, and one that often took hours, for it meant trampling the snow sufficiently hard with your heavy snow-shoes for the dogs to have firm ground beneath their feet and to be able to pull the sledge back on to the track, which, though it might be covered with soft snow, did have a hard bottom.

Because of that I kept to the track as far as I possibly could and would not let myself be enticed off if it could be avoided. Nobody would, and that fact often cost you hours on a good sledging day, when you were halted amid furious scurries of angry words by encountering an oncoming sledge on the track: which of you was to give way and get out into the soft impassable snow at the side, he or you?

Tales were told in Alaska of frequent recourse being had to revolvers to settle that question, and I could understand it only too well, for I was myself tempted, though I did remain content to let my vocabulary and Jutlander's pigheadedness decide the issue. I remember one incredibly cold day with the sun shining and no wind, wonderful sledging weather when you can keep warm by running beside the sledge, and how I cursed when I met an oncoming sledge and had to halt.

The leaders stood rigid like statues, muzzle to muzzle, snarling and growling, but realizing from experience that the situation called for calm, they soon lay down, tucked their noses under their tails and went to sleep in the sunshine. They left it to those with two legs to decide which was to give way. To begin with we talked nicely, discussing who should, or ought to, get off the track, the one emphasizing the great weight of his own sledge and the rest of it, which the other immediately countered, alleging that his sledge was much heavier, dogs worse and far more tired. It was a duel of words in which you could use many arguments, as we did, but we might just as well have spared ourselves the trouble and the insults we heaped upon each other, for ordinary arguments would not get either of us into the deep snow at the side, and though some of the insults were hair-raising, they were both mutual and without effect.

The result was the usual one of our falling silent, sitting down on our sledges, lighting our pipes and glaring at each other, hoping to be able to freeze the other off the track. That was a process that could be a lengthy one if both were wearing warm furs, though it could prove quite quick if your opponent was new in the country and had not yet had an opportunity to acquire proper furs. On that incredibly cold day I spent three long hours sitting on my sledge, freezing abominably but determined not to give in, for my opponent was even colder than I and imprudent enough to show it by trying to slap warmth into his body. Eventually, scowling angrily, but still not saying a word, he tied on his snow-shoes and began tramping a little track to the side; to and fro he trod, to and fro many times to make it hard enough to bear the dogs and sledge. And when, in the end he whipped up his dogs and got going, I gave him a grim smile, wished him a good journey and better luck the next time he met an oncoming sledge. But he did not appreciate my courtesy—or perhaps he was so angry he did not hear what I said.

Every fifteen or twenty miles along this endless track which wound like a snake without head or tail all the way across Alaska from Candle City to Valdez, was a hut where tired or exhausted sledgers could find shelter for the night, or wait while a storm raged itself out. Some of those guest-huts were large and good, others tiny, stuffy and overcrowded, but one thing at least they had in common, that they were run as a rule by people who had come to the country with great expectations of getting rich quick, but had been knocked out of the running either by not being able to stand up to the life or else by general disappointment, and so had been compelled to abandon their hopes of easy money. Thus they were all embittered men.

There was one other characteristic these owners of Alaska's guest-huts, both big and small, had in common, they took as good payment for a night's lodging and provisions as a wayfarer could possibly be asked to pay. The better off he was, the more they asked. But even the worst off, he who came trudging along the endless track on foot with his few possessions in a sack on his back and death at his side, even he had to pay and pay dear, before he was allowed to lean his tired back against the rough-hewn logs of the hut or was given a piece of bread.

But these inns, or roadhouses as they were called, could also be pleasant places, and in them you met all kinds of people. There was the lucky gold-digger who came driving up in a magnificent sledge with a team of ten dogs, and quite often more, with bells jingling on their harness, lovely to hear in quiet frosty weather, and useful for calling people out from the roadhouse long before the great man arrived, so that he could be received as was fit and proper.

The great one would be made to pay through the nose as he deserved to be, but it was all the same to him. He had struck lucky and would just chuck a bag of gold dust on to the table: 'Landlord, I'm hungry, bring food!' 'Landlord, I'm thirsty, give me—give everybody a drink, and the most expensive you have.'

There was more quietness about the unlucky man who came trudging up with a team of a few thin dogs, on his way from one broken hope to another, as he chased his dream of gold about that huge country. He had not yet been knocked right out, and still spoke big of what he would do when he found his bonanza away beyond the mountains which you could see, blue with distance, against the blue of the sky, far, far away, where no busy men had yet dug down to bed-rock. Why shouldn't he, despite previous bad luck, not strike lucky in the end?

And there came a man you had perhaps already swept past in a cloud of snow as despondently he trudged his weary solitary way, stepping aside into the deep snow to give the more fortunate room to pass, perhaps in the hope that you, in arrogant consciousness of your greatness, would stop and say to him: 'Get up and come with me, we're both going the same way!' That man had no dogs, no sledge, no illusions, no hope, for the blindfold goddess had failed him everywhere where others had drawn a prize. And now he was too poor to be able to leave the country, as well as too poor to live in it. His only course was to trudge on and on, to go on walking till he collapsed on to the track, and the snow covered him, a hidden and forgotten man, one of the great army which disappeared in Alaska in the hectic years of the gold rush. Many of them had courage enough to put a bullet through their heads, and one of whom I heard had sufficient macabre humour first to pin a paper to his chest on which he had written: 'Hell cannot be worse than this country. I prefer hell.'

There too you could meet the tenderfoot, who lapped down what the old hands told him as a kitten does milk, believing every word that was said and standing expensive drinks in the hope that tipsy men would reveal to him, the newcomer, where the fountain-head of riches was to be found. But lies and invention was about all he ever got for his money.

In the roadhouses you could also meet the tough team-drivers who drove the US post sledge from Valdez to Nome, young men, magnificent dog drivers, who changed teams every thirty miles or so and drove across country at such speed no one could keep up with them, covering sixty miles a day, perhaps more. They were awaited with excitement, those postilions of the Fates, bringers of good or evil tidings, who left joy or sorrow behind them, when, after a brief rest in the roadhouse, they disappeared like heavenly beings in a cloud of snow.

You also saw women at the roadhouses, but not often, which

was a good thing, as their presence completely altered the free and easy atmosphere of those male paradises, where there was usually only the one resident woman, the owner's wife, or perhaps someone come to console him in his loneliness and who also attended to all the woman's duties there—but such did not count. The women who travelled the sledge-trail through Alaska were as a rule only of two kinds: the one had a revolver on her thigh, hard sharp gaze and tight-clamped mouth, a tough and strong-willed woman who was out to find gold and was ready to sacrifice the same as the male prospectors to get it. Each of her movements, the expression on her face, each of her few words, and the revolver at her belt said most distinctly: Touch me if you dare!

A hush would fall over the roadhouse when one of these women stepped in, and the men, otherwise so outspoken, would bridle their tongues, talk politely and softly, glancing at the woman in the hope of finding a chink in the armour in which she had clad herself. But there was seldom any such chink to be seen, even more seldom a half-promising smile: she minded her own business and by sheer force of character curbed those who were usually so unbridled.

At night she shared the same sleeping quarters as the rest of the occupants of the roadhouse, and though individually they may have thought all sorts of things, they kept their thoughts to themselves, and you scarcely heard any of the usual uninhibited noises of the night.

She came to the roadhouse for rest, food and warmth, and she went on her way again either on foot or by sledge as soon as conditions allowed, followed to the door by wondering, subdued men who with a smile half stupid, half apologetic at having been cowed by a woman, would spit out a long jet of saliva and watch her go. When she was well away and no longer able to hear what they said, a chorus of gruff voices with a note of admiration in them would exclaim: 'What the hell of a woman!'

The other kind of woman who came to the roadhouse was one who always drove as one of the great ones, with bells on her dogs' harness and a sledge covered with fur; lissom and soft and smiling she would be, always dressed in the finest furs, with rings on her fingers and bit of jewellery here and there.

She would be greeted joyfully and her presence bridled no man's tongue nor paralysed his actions. Food appeared on the table, the best the house could produce, and drink flowed in streams round the beauty. She would accept the boisterous homage of the men with smiles and laughter and playful ingratiating words, yet usually these would be addressed only to those who appeared to be the grandees of Gold-Digger Land and who were footing the bill. We others would be weighed with a glance and found too light in the purse.

And of course there would be squabbling or a row: why him and not me? But the beauty—though not all were equally beautiful —would just gaze at the flock of the despised with a Mona Lisa smile, and feast with the one—or more—of the elect, promising all and keeping her promises.

When she moved on, usually in the company of a grandee, the men would also follow her to the door and spit out long jets on to the white snow, unless they were too busy unburdening themselves of all the not very complimentary remarks they had had on the tips of their tongues all the while she was at the roadhouse and which they wanted her to hear before she left. And when she disappeared down the track in a swirl of snow, the men would all loudly agree that she was the hell of a woman!

But it would be contempt, not admiration you could hear in their voices.

The women of that sort did well on the sledge-route between Valdez and Nome, especially on the stretches which ran through the sheltering forest where the roadhouses stood thick. It was all the same to them whether they sledged towards the north or the south, for they were at home wherever there were men, and although they were not gold-prospectors as such and could scarcely boast of doing an honest day's work, they were gold-hunters and raked it in by the bag and the sack.

I too stayed at those roadhouses, but only as a foreign bird of passage migrating south and an object of astonishment. What, they wondered, had this man who was not interested in gold wanted up there in Alaska? For the people of Nome had seen to it that all the owners of the roadhouses along the trail to Valdez should know about me. After a long day's sledging I was unaffectedly glad of the warmth and the rest the roadhouse afforded, and looked forward to sitting in the friendly company of a chance gathering of all sorts, and I enjoyed listening to their tales of gold, countries and people, and was always glad of a report on the route I should be following when the next day dawned: was it good or bad, easy to follow or hidden beneath a covering of snow?

Those roadhouses were news exchanges, manufactories of rumours, where every report was turned inside out and retold until it was unrecognizable—as were those about myself and my absurd search for land north of Alaska. What was the point of such foolery?

You heard about each man on the route long before he reached the roadhouse, or long after he had left it. You heard about the lucky gold-digger, whose luck was multiplied by envious fellow-devotees of the goddess Fortune, and about the unlucky, the poor ones, whose bad luck and wretchedness were usually made out worse than they actually were, hard and bitter though the reality might be.

Every new arrival at a roadhouse brought news with him, good or bad; whether true or not was of little significance, as long as you had something to tell which the others had not heard, otherwise you were a 'bad chum.' You heard rumours of huge finds made in districts so far away that the rumour could neither be confirmed nor disproved, but however distant they were they lured the fortune-hunters out on a highly dangerous and usually most unrewarding journey.

You heard of small towns which had grown up here and there on the mere rumour of gold, and then been abandoned abruptly when after months of hoping and toiling industrious men had reached bedrock without even a gleam of gold being seen. You heard too of disappointments in the hunt for gold so heavy that a man could not bear them, but sent a bullet into his brain at the bottom of some shaft when empty bedrock had grinned at him shattering his hopes. And you heard of the tenderfoot who had pooh-poohed all warnings not to seek his fortune in Alaska and who had been found sitting beside the sledge-track, cold and dead, frozen to death, before he had even learned to get along in that stern land or even set spade to the ground.

They told tales of highwaymen on the trail, desperate men who wanted to have gold without too much work. You had to beware of them, especially if you were a grandee with a jingling bell-strung dog-team harnessed to your sledge and gold-dust in great big bags of elk-skin. For highwaymen—like no few of the old hands in Alaska—could use a revolver, could shoot a hole in the ace of spades in a card thrown up into the air. That was a popular pastime in the larger roadhouses, but one not unfraught with danger where it was indulged in by half-inebriated, boastful men, who all insisted that they could shoot better than other people, even without hitting the ace of spades.

You heard tales of ferocious grizzly bears attacking unsuspecting travellers, and of wolves following people's trails for days and creeping up so close to their camp-fires that the watchful could take aim at their eyes glowing where the firelight wrestled with the darkness. And an apparently thoroughly reliable man asserted one evening that once, when without a rifle, he had been forced to sit all day on his sledge while a huge bull elk—the bulls can be very dangerous—which had emerged out of the soft snow, had asserted his unchallenged right to priority and strolled lazily along the hard-trodden trail halting all traffic.

You heard many kinds of rumours and stories when you spent the night in a roadhouse. Some were true, but others, and they no doubt the majority, were lies and sheer invention, and those must often have caused credulous men to die an early death by luring them on to false scents and sending them to search for gold in the wilds hundreds of miles off the beaten track.

165

But one tale I never heard all the time I was sledging was that of the silly man who carried another man's gold across hill and dale, hidden at the bottom of a kitbag which lay on his sledge by day and by night, so easy to rip up with a sharp sheath knife if anyone had known.

The rash shopkeeper in Nome had of course kept his mouth shut, and that silly man only remembered the gold when the going was heavy and the gradient so steep that he had to curse his stupid helpfulness, and would gladly have left the gold where he and his sledge stuck.

When a storm blew up while you were snug and comfortable in a roadhouse and especially if it lasted two or three days, the impatient men gradually found themselves hard up for topics of conversation and would then have recourse in their desperation to a special Alaskan parlour-game: swopping tall stories. They were good at that, those men on long sledging treks, so inventive that a novice in the art of lying had to sit quiet and listen with mouth agape. Each one individually did his best, and astounding assertions about 'quite true' occurrences here and there were produced, the more amazing the better.

I remember one evening at the end of a three days' storm. There were a lot of people in the roadhouse who all knew what it was to freeze, and they produced some astounding stories about cold. I was only a bird of passage in the country and not so practised in the art, so when my turn came I told the entirely true tale of the fools in ordinary clothes I had met in Death Valley and who had frozen to death in their senseless search for gold. I made it as dramatic as I could, and I thought I had done it quite well and that it contained a sound moral which many of my audience would have done well to mark and inwardly digest. The story, however, fell completely flat, and one grey-haired and widely-travelled gold-digger—at least he himself said that he was, but that perhaps was a lie too—just shook his head and looked at me pityingly: 'Have you really never experienced anything worse than that on your travels? What you have just told us happens over and over again up here in this god-forsaken Alaska and is not worth mentioning among men.'

'But you see,' went on that widely travelled man, 'in this damned country I have experienced cold so fierce that one evening instead of blowing my candle out when I went to bed, I broke the flame off and chucked it out of the door. And the flame was so cold that it didn't even splutter as it sank quietly into the snow.

'You see, boys, it's only when you've experienced something like that, and I have as I've told you, that you can talk about cold.'

No one could cap that story, and a hush fell upon the roadhouse, while each wondered what next he could produce.

You could have a really pleasant time on a journey through Alaska, and you learned a lot about people and countries by listening to experienced men telling their tales in the roadhouses, while the storms wrestled with the house and made it shake like an aspen.

And then you drank to pass the time, drank hard, and the owner was kept busy serving his expensive drinks, for which he didn't ask minted coin or dollar bills, in fact, he preferred to be paid in gold dust and the finer the better.

He loved gold; after all, it was his love of gold which had taken him there in the first place, for good or evil. And so he fondled the gold, thrust his hands deep in the big elk-skin bags with the fine dust, took out a handful and let it trickle through his fingers so that it glittered in the light: lovely gold dust! Then he carefully weighed out what he was due for his drinks on a sensitive pair of scales and poured the rest of the gold back into the bag, giving the little pan of the scales a good shake so that not a grain of gold was left on it. He was an honest man, you see.

Yet behind the counter there stood two pails, one filled with a thin sticky liquid, the other with clear water, and each time the man had fingered gold dust he swished his hands round in the water and the fine but heavy dust sank to the bottom, and before he weighed the next lot of gold-dust he dipped his hands into the sticky fluid—syrup-water was good for the purpose.

The owner of a guest-house would entrust the weighing of gold-dust to no one; if his nails were long, as they usually were, a lot of gold could hide there. And if Nature had endowed him with nice hairy hands, he was just made for the job.

It must have been a lucrative business being owner of a road-house and weighing out the gold-dust with which to pay yourself. That must certainly have brought in more than what you made on food and drink, though that profit can't have been so small either.

CHAPTER XVI

GOLD

The effect of sun and calm on sledgers—A strange way of living—
Reluctant hosts become friendly—Gold by the bucket—Fort Gibbon

IT WAS a long way to Valdez and as stopping at roadhouses was expensive I usually stayed no longer than I had to, but pressed on as soon as the weather made travelling possible.

I sledged across long treeless stretches over which the wind swept, whipping the snow up into huge blinding clouds. It felt snug and cosy when the trail led through forest which broke the force of the wind, and I enjoyed such sledging in shelter from which you could see the wind playing with an eagle despite its powerful wings and forcing the tall crests of the trees to bow deep.

If the weather was calm and the sun shining from a cloudless sky, which was not so seldom as you might think, I would halt my team and, despite the cold, let eye and mind feast quietly on the beauty of the rime-powdered birches and spruces glistening and silhouetted against the deep-blue sky. It was a sight of such unearthly beauty that even hardened 'mushers' at times felt as though they had been transported to a wondrous fairyland.

Softly the rime would fall from twigs and branches powdering me with sparkling crystals which settled on the sledge and all that I had on it—it even improved the look of my kitbag, making it more beautiful than all the gold there was inside. And it settled thickly on my faithful dogs who enjoyed the rest after a hard run. Their breath hovered above them like small rainbow-coloured clouds, making it appear as if each of the panting dogs had a halo round his head.

The splendours of Nature would put you in so peaceable a mood that if an oncoming sledge appeared while you were enjoying the sight of them, you might find yourself being friendly to its driver: 'Lovely isn't it, stranger? Glorious day—now let me help you trample a track round.'

And he would nod: 'You're right, friend, it's grand in Alaska. Look at that birch tree, so white, so gleaming, as virgin as a young bride; and look at that dark spruce in its finery, like a respectable matron celebrating her silver wedding. But you are tired; I can see you've come far; so rest friend, and I'll tread the track myself, the snow's not so deep today. But first let's have a smoke and a bit of a chat. It gets a bit melancholy just talking to the dogs the live-long day.'

Then you would discuss the trail; he telling about that along which he had come, you about the stretch ahead of him; then you talked about the roadhouses which lay behind you both, saying which were good and bad, and about the people you had met in them. And perhaps a wistful look would come into the other's eye when he remembered some of those with whom he had once spent a night: 'There was a girl there in Goldcreek Roadhouse, you know, one of the proper sort. But she was with a man just stuffed with gold, and naturally she never looked at me. Blast him—and her too!'

It might happen that you too had just recently met a girl in one of the roadhouses, and then the talk would turn of itself on to the sex, which though the weaker, could easily twist us round its little finger if it wanted—and we possessed gold and not just youth alone.

Sitting on your sledges enjoying a chat, however, did not bring either of you any nearer your destinations, so, after discussing this and that, you had to get on and in amicable harmony you trod the track broader till there was room for the two sledges to pass.

I left one such encounter with a warning about a nasty steep slope to which I would shortly be coming: 'It's pretty severe, you know,' I was told, 'but remember the Spaniard. I hope he's at home when you get to the mountain.'

The Spaniard? I had not heard of him before, but I was reluctant to admit ignorance of what was obviously a well-known phenomenon of the trail, for after all I was a 'musher' (sledge-driver) like everyone else in Alaska, almost an old-timer, so I just nodded my thanks and said that I hoped so too.

With cracks of my whip and a volley of oaths I got the dogs on their feet and pulling again, and off I jingled southwards down the trail wondering to myself what or whom the Spaniard might be and also where he came in.

I soon found out. Ahead of me was the steep mountainside and the trail which seemed to be leading up into the sky. I shrank from the thought of the climb and remembered the deadweight in my kitbag; it would probably be a job driving the dogs up that seemingly perpendicular trail. But no doubt it would turn out all right, as everything else had on my long journey—and then I encountered the Spaniard, sitting in a temperature of thirty or forty degrees below freezing outside his house, smiling complacently and letting himself be baked by the sun.

I did not know that it was he and just waved a greeting with my whip, while I squinted up at the trail, which from close to looked even more perpendicular than it had from a distance; then I said a word or two to the man who still sat sunning himself, and whipped up the dogs; but though I cursed them a bit to get them really going as we started the ascent, we soon stuck fast. The dogs could not manage it. Again and again the whip whined over them, again and again I affronted Nature by using a mass of words which did not belong in those lovely surroundings. But it was all no use; the outlook was rather grim, and I glared furiously at my kitbag, as I had so many times already; should I translate threats into action and really leave the contents behind? That would lighten the sledge more than a little.

Suddenly the man I had just driven past was standing beside me: 'I'm the Spaniard,' he said, and laughed.

'And so what?' said I, for I was irritated and in no mood to be friendly to the grinning man. I would rather have smashed my first into his face to wipe that beastly smile off it; if I had been alone in my defeat, it perhaps would not have felt so bad, but that

I, an old and experienced musher should be made a fool of by sticking on a bit of a slope was well nigh intolerable. It was both degrading and ignominious!

Resentment lent strength to my arm: the whip whined again and the dogs did their very best, but it was no use. The sledge might have been nailed to the trail.

'I am the Spaniard,' came the voice of the smiling man at my side mildly enough, 'Shall I help you?'

'What with?' I asked, inwardly furious, and, taking another grip on the sledge, I whipped the dogs so that they yelped and their feet went like drum-sticks: 'How will you help me?'

'By doing what you can't do!' said the Spaniard sarcastically, 'drive your sledge up the hill here. You won't manage it if you try till Hell freezes. You must be new in this country if you don't know me—so my help will cost you a bit more than usual—and also because you drove past me so arrogantly, when you still thought you were no end of a fine fellow and could easily drive a sledge up the mountain. I am not accustomed to that, all experienced mushers know me—and the mountain, which you won't be able to get up.'

I looked at the smiling man with the Spanish-looking face and the queer accent. Did he really think he could get it going where I had stuck? That made me really angry, and I told the Spaniard to go to Hell and clear out, and all the rest of the things you say without necessarily meaning them to be taken literally. He had done nothing to me, except to grin when I didn't feel like laughing. Nor did he clear off despite my angry words, but just stood there and laughed and jeered now and again with sharp little gibes which cut me to the quick.

But our wrangling did not get me to the top. After trying again and again, I flung down the traces, wiped the sweat and the rime off my face and off the long hair of my furs and said: 'All right, you try then!'

'Gladly,' said he and laughed, 'but first your money;' so we haggled about that, and eventually agreed on a price which wasn't a small one. I was still sufficient of a sailor to honour the old ship's practice: no pay, no cure! The Spaniard did not know that, but when I had explained it to him and he had seen for himself that I really had the money, we settled on half the amount he had had the presumption to ask in the first place.

He went and got his own whip, which was decidedly better and heavier than mine, and when he gave it a couple of cracks the sound of it made the dogs look round in surprise; then he picked up the traces—and loosed a flood of oaths the like of which I had never heard; and each oath seemed to act on the dogs like a stinging lash with a whip. It was amazing. I had thought that I knew quite a lot about oaths, but it was obvious that I still had a great deal to learn. And the dogs began pulling again with fresh strength and increased energy; the sledge shook, gave a short jerk forwards, was moving—while oaths flashed through the air like lightning and the whip was never still for an instant. To the accompaniment of cracks on the whip like pistol shots and oaths which would have congealed the blood in your veins, the sledge slid slowly up the mountainside, and I walked along behind, amazed and envious, and wondering where the Spaniard had acquired his fantastic vocabulary.

But we got to the top all right, and there he halted, threw down the traces and laughed: 'That was a tussle! Your sledge is heavier than I had judged—what have you got on it? Well, that doesn't concern me, a bargain's a bargain. Give me the money, and if you come this way again, you'll know me the next time.'

He got his money, and he had really earned every cent of it. We began talking, and I learned that in a couple of years or so he had made quite a bit by infusing new strength into dog-teams with the oaths he had brought from the land of his birth, or wherever it was he had acquired them. It was a queer occupation, and a queer country which had use for powers which would have had no value in gentler parts.

They were certainly not boring people you met on the sledge trail between Nome and Valdez.

One day I was caught by some really dirty weather. The ditch with the trodden track at the bottom of it was drifted full of soft snow, into which the sledge sank deep and so even did the dogs, and I had to trudge along where I thought the trail was with snowshoes on my feet. The dogs were tired and unco-operative, I was exhausted and bad-tempered, so we made a miserable lot, and there was little prospect of getting along any better until the weather changed. Then the dogs got the scent of a house, and shortly afterwards through the swirling snow I saw a little hut, not one of the ordinary roadhouses, but obviously a miner's hut.

When we reached it the dogs did not need to be told that their day's work was over: they flung themselves down in the snow and I set about getting the harness off them. While I was doing that I could not help feeling surprised that no one came out to see who was pottering about out there in the storm. People always came out when strangers arrived, if for no other reason than curiosity. And the hut was inhabited, that was quite obvious, because smoke was pouring from the chimney and the snow had been shovelled away from the door. They must be a pretty queer lot inside, I told myself.

When at last I had finished with the dogs, and still no one had appeared, I strode across to the door intending just to walk in. I was feeling pretty angry with the occupants for their lack of hospitality, which in those parts was mostly held in high honour and practised, visitors being few and as a rule welcome, if only because of the news and rumours they brought.

But these people were decidedly most uninquisitive and very in-hospitable, for when I opened the door there inside stood a young man holding a rifle at the ready and saying: 'Hop it, stranger, or I shoot!'

I told him that there was nothing I should have liked better than to have been able to drive on, but drew his attention to the filthy weather, the tired state of my dogs, the hard going, and I may perhaps also have said a word or two about that being the first time I had met with an unfriendly reception all the long way from Nome. However the man insisted: 'Get out, or I'll shoot!'

We parleyed for quite a while. It was cold, and we both got rather angry. A second man appeared in the doorway, as young as the other, and joined in our battle of words; he was not friendly, but certainly not as unsympathetic as his companion. In the end, after a lot of palaver, they allowed me inside, and I seated myself sulkily in a corner. Then, never saying a word, I ferreted some food out of my bag and ate it, glaring at the other two, who sat by a crackling fire talking together in whispers.

When we settled down for the night, I noticed that the two men took their rifles into their bunks with them, and, as there was no knowing what they had in mind, I quite openly laid my revolver beside my sleeping bag. If there was going to be shooting, I intended to take part too.

Outside, the storm was howling worse than ever; it wailed and moaned in all the cracks and holes in the walls of the hut, its notes ranging from high falsetto to booming bass. Now and again I heard the dogs complaining bitterly, but I did not dare go out to see to them, as I was afraid that my hosts would bar the door on me. I stayed where I was, keeping myself awake as much as possible, since the others were taking it in turns to stay awake.

If it was grim outside, it was also grim inside. That was a long and unpleasant night.

The next morning the weather was as bad as ever, if not worse, and I said meekly: 'I would be glad to get away, but I can't in this weather.' One of the young men replied curtly: 'Who's saying you should?' And at the same time he shoved a large mug of steaming coffee towards me: 'It's been a long night; you'll need coffee as much as we.'

The ice was broken, and being all young, we were soon talking. My inhospitable hosts proved to be not so bad after all, and even better the next night, when they left their rifles hanging on the wall, and I shoved my revolver out of reach. The following morning we were friends; we laughed and joked and we together went out to feed my dogs with the young men's provisions, for I had none on my sledge. The weather was worse than ever.

By the third day we had become friends for life; and also we had learned a great deal about each other. Of me my hosts knew, amongst other things, that I was a foreign bird of passage and not in the least interested in gold. In that respect they made up for me. The jumble of gold-digger's gear which littered the hut told its own story—and towards evening, when the weather had improved slightly, they said to me: 'Come and look!'

We went out of the hut and down a little path through the dense forest till we came to a tent erected over a gaping hole—a shaft. Into this my friends lowered a ladder they had taken with them; and while one clambered down and invited me to follow him, the other stood guard at the top with his rifle at the ready.

At the bottom of that shaft I saw a sight I had never seen before nor since: two square kerosene tins, one almost full of gold, the other half full: 'Now you will understand,' said my friend in the shaft, as he let the light play across that golden treasure, 'why strangers are not welcome here. They might easily get ideas!'

I could understand that only too well, and for a moment even I felt that it would have been nice if only I could have found a bonanza like that. But it was only a fleeting thought, which passed through my head and was gone. I had my joys and expectations, they theirs, and the difference between them was enormous. It might well be that mine were greater and would last longer than any my new friends could buy with all their gold. But I'm not denying that—for a moment—the temptation to try gold-digging was great.

My leave-taking from the two young occupants of the hut was thus very different from my reception; and while I drove on along the trail enjoying the sunshine, the loveliness of the country and the purity of the air, with my head full of dreams about future journeys and expeditions, the two solitary men descended into their dark shaft and continued scraping gold-bearing sand out of the unevenness in the bedrock, washing out the fine gold dust in huge pans, toiling and labouring to increase their treasure. I wonder how much joy and happiness it brought them?

I struggled along the trail in all weathers, sometimes in bright sunshine, which made the rime on the gossamer of the birch trees twigs and branches and the frozen snow on the dark spruces glisten and sparkle, as though they were strewn with diamonds and precious stones; sometimes in storm and swirling snow so thick I could not see my hand in front of me, but staggered about blindly, getting in among trees and bushes that caught and tangled the dogs' harness, which I then had to disentangle with bare hands in the stinging cold. On some days I covered a wonderful distance, on others it was shamefully short. I spent the nights in the road-houses, some of which were good, others pretty wretched, or else in the shanties of the soldiers who looked after the telegraph lines, which were always kept fine and clean. I sought shelter where I could find it, sometimes even with the Indians, but they had learned far too much from their white masters. They were any-thing but obliging to those who travelled the trail, and though they lived in such miserable huts that they scarcely deserved the name, they usually demanded for a night's board and lodging three times as much as the most expensive roadhouse.

One day, when I had been more than a month on the trail since leaving Nome, I drove, harness bells jingling and whip cracking, into Fort Gibbon. Fort Gibbon was the nerve centre of Alaska from where a hundred soldiers maintained the telegraph line and bravely tried to impart a semblance of law and order to that fairly lawless country. It was less a fort than a town of one long street and, fronting the wilderness, a number of large and spacious buildings with officers' quarters and roomy offices, in which busy men swept papers about and administered Alaska, worthy representatives of the might and power of the USA with its love of administration.

There were hospitals too, as many as three, I think, and parade grounds for the troops on which the snow was deep and smooth and untouched, so their training must have been restricted to the summer half of the year. That, at least, is what I thought then, but even that wasn't right, for later I met people who had been to Fort Gibbon in the summer, and they had found the parade grounds just as empty and untrodden as I had. That started us off grumbling and wondering whether they took training and that sort of thing seriously, or whether they weren't rather inclined to forget standing orders and regulations when they got up there.

There was also a barracks for the troops and some public baths, and where the official buildings came to an end, the unofficial lay huddled just anyhow: a dozen pubs, a proper restaurant and a hotel, a comparatively large department store where you could buy anything if you had money or 'dust' enough; a couple of less elegant establishments, where all sorts of illicit trading flourished more or less openly right in the citadel of law and order; some private dwelling houses for the civilian population, and then the town ended in a building set athwart the street like an awful warning to the unruly who might be upon it. This was the prison which was reputed to have a larger population than all the rest of the little town, soldiers included.

I had had a telegram some time before inviting me to be the guest of Major Clifton, commandant of the Fort, and so, after a bath and all that goes with that when you haven't had a bath for months, I dressed in my best, which was no longer much to write home about, and went to see the major and his wife, a grand couple who took me to their hearts and made my stay in Fort Gibbon most enjoyable.

After that long sledge journey I really was in need of a rest before I tackled the final stretch to Valdez, and so I allowed myself ten days during which I enjoyed being a civilized being, and forgot all the difficulties of the journey, leaving myself with only its joys to remember. And they had been many. Then I again put on my sledging clothes, harnessed my dogs to the sledge, cracked my whip, which I now did with an air, though not quite as well as the Spaniard had wielded his, and was back on the trail once more. As soon as it reached the far side of the huge River Yukon it plunged into true virgin country with great forests and deep snow, and there I met many travellers as well as hopeful plodders trudging along in answer to the magic call of gold and expecting to find great heaps of the yellow metal behind each of the many bends in the trail.

CHAPTER XVII

THE HECTIC LIFE OF THE
GOLD COUNTRY

*Sullivan Creek—A gold town—Diamond Jim—an encounter on the trail—
An optimist from Kentucky—Fairbanks and its glories—A town celebrates
—The optimist abandons hope*

I WAS now making for Sullivan City, a gold-digger town which
was rumoured to be one huge bonanza. There, only that autumn,
lucky gold-hungry men had begun quarrying the frozen ground
with dynamite and gunpowder, using huge bonfires to thaw it
out so that they could shovel the earth with its gold out of the
shafts they had sunk.

I had heard so much and so often about Sullivan that I was
expecting a lot, but even so I was astounded by what I saw as I
drove into it, that 'town' which was only six or seven months old.
News of the rich finds made there had spread on the wings of the
wind all over Alaska and far into America. Men, and women too,
kept pouring in. People laboured in the frozen ground all day and
half the night as well, blasting, digging, thawing the ground with
the heat of hundreds and hundreds of fires, toiling and sweating
for a month or two until they got down to bedrock where as
often as not bitter disappointment awaited them as their only
reward.

But some, no many, were lucky and had their inhuman toil
rewarded, yet their gains were never so big that rumour did not
multiply them as it spread the news about the land, so that more
and more fortune-seekers flocked there. Sellers of provisions and
equipment came and set up tents to house their precious wares;
at first perhaps only a few tins of baking powder, some sacks of
flour and beans, a little bacon—then considerably more, but
however much, it was all brought the hundred miles overland
from Valdez partly on sledges and half the way on men's backs.

Everything found a rapid sale, for all who could wanted to buy.

While goods poured in at one end of the trader's tent, they were snapped up at the other by the lucky ones who hastened to lay in a good store so as not to be halted by lack of provisions and equipment.

The unlucky ones were there too, and for a wage of ten dollars or so an hour, they helped transport the fortunate ones' purchases back to the many gold-bearing shafts which were scattered far and wide, or else they tried to earn enough to enable them to start again by felling big trees for building relatively permanent shops and stores, which were always too small for their purpose long before they were finished. So then they built more. There were plenty of trees, and plenty of unlucky gold-diggers whom necessity compelled to ply axe, saw and hammer for a while instead of pick, shovel and spade. Buildings shot up like mushrooms, some of them just wretched hovels, others quite big houses—but one and all had room for a bar, which remained open round the clock so that hard-working men could quench their mighty thirst in excessively dear spirits, served by barmen with long nails and hairy hands, and provided with the two buckets which were just as essential a part of a bar-tender's equipment in Gold-digger Land as the bottles from which he poured his fiery drinks.

Day and night there were always diggers drinking, either celebrating a rich find or drowning a bitter disappointment, perhaps even acquiring fresh courage to enable them to start all over again. Many drank till they had no money left and had to take to servile toil with axe, saw and hammer—or else get out, off down the pitiless trail, where they might yet be lucky enough to hear a true report of a new find elsewhere, or perhaps encounter a compassionate Samaritan, easier to find there than in a hectic new mining town.

Girls came to the town as soon as they could get a roof over their heads, and at a pinch they would make do with a tent. Dance halls were one of the first things to be built, and splendid names they were given. 'Moulin Rouge' was all the fashion in those days, and you would see the name painted up in garish colours outside, and inside some shipwrecked artist would have found an outlet for his genius by painting the diggers' ideal woman on the walls with a coarse brush. This was usually a wild and passionate Amazon who wasn't so particular about clothes and that sort of thing, but showed her charms, both here and there.

The phonographs and mechanical pianos of those early days blared and bellowed their artificial *joie de vivre* over land and forest; drunken men fought with bare fists, encouraged and incited by the loud shouts of the spectators; half-drunken girls shrieked or laughed hysterically; an ear-splitting noise rose up far into the deep-blue sky and could be heard for miles across the snow-covered ground enticing the diggers away from their laborious work, scaring the wild animals of the forest and driving them to quieter parts, where the lords of creation had not yet set up their noisy tents.

Sullivan Creek, however, was said to be by no means the worst or the noisiest of the gold-digger towns, because not far away was a large hotel which was the haunt of all who could afford to pay and pay well. It was called Hot Springs, and it absorbed one-third of Sullivan's noisy population. The hotel did boast a few bedsteads, but most of the two and three-storeyed building was occupied by gambling room, restaurant and dance-hall, not forgetting a large bar. In fact, Hot Springs Hotel could provide all that the heart desired or a wild man of the woods could require after six months in the solitude of the wilds.

The owner of all those splendours, who was said to have been given the name of Manley at his baptism, was known all over Alaska as Diamond Jim.

It was a strange nickname in that gold country where there wasn't a diamond to be found; but Diamond Jim wanted to show off by having that which was more precious even than gold, and so in order to flaunt his wealth before God and Everyman, wealth which he had partly acquired by digging, but mostly no doubt by entertaining tipsy men whose pockets were bulging with gold dust when they came to his hotel and empty when they left it, Diamond

Jim always wore a cap on which was a gold brooch set with a large diamond.

It was no wonder that Diamond Jim always kept his precious cap on his head when he was at home in Alaska, but if one can believe rumour, he had great difficulty in looking after it when he was on holiday in San Francisco where people were said to be even more light-fingered than in Alaska.

Diamond Jim was not bad looking; he was a magnificent figure, a gigantic Irishman with a fist so large that even the strongest digger would give way respectfully if Jim showed signs of taking his coat off. And it was said to be a well-known fact that drunken customers, who otherwise feared neither God nor the devil, became painfully sober when Diamond Jim made it clear that he would attend to them in person. But things had to be really bad before he did that.

Diamond Jim invited me to live in his fine hotel, where I shared a room and a bed with two or three gold-diggers; they, however, were seldom in the room, for there were greater attractions than me to be found elsewhere in that large building.

Boring my stay there certainly was not, for I met those who had tales to tell which it was a joy to hear, yet I did not feel properly in sympathy with the strange crowd of both sexes, whom you would find at all hours of the day and night dancing round the golden calf of Hot Springs, relieving the real diggers of so much of their hard-won wealth that they were often unable to pay Diamond Jim what they owed for food and drink and their entertainment.

As a rule, of course, Diamond Jim could tell pretty well what each man in the hotel was worth when he first came in, and he always took the news with great equanimity. Every such failure gave him an opportunity to take a mortgage or a share in his debtor's gold mine, so that sooner or later he recovered the amount of his bill and more.

Once again I set off down the endless trail, now a hard-trodden road which wound through forests of tall trees. Virgin though the forest was, there was not always shelter from storm and drifting snow, for great havoc had been wrought in it by the camp-fires people had built along the trail. Now, there were places where you could sledge for mile after mile along stretches where the trees had been burned down by thoughtless travellers leaving big fires blazing when they broke camp, which had then set fire to the forest. Many square miles of what had been virgin forest were covered with nothing but scorched and blackened trunks, silent witnesses to man's thoughtlessness and wastefulness with Nature's resources in that rich land of gold and timber.

Many people too must have lost their lives when the forest took fire, and flames and acrid smoke came up and surrounded men tired with long marches in pursuit of their golden hopes.

Alaska, however, had no lack of men, and still more kept pouring in. I met many of them along the trail, walking, sledging behind horse or dogs, even riding on old nags which must have cost their tired but proud riders more than any thoroughbred in a rich man's stable.

Anything might happen when you travelled that trail, and one evening when it was so late that I had to give up the idea of going on to the next roadhouse, I came upon a man sitting, well satisfied with life, in front of a little tent pitched by the side of the track. He had a large fire burning, and kept feeding it with good thick branches which crackled and sent a shower of sparks and blazing particles spurting up into the black night sky.

You could see at once that he was an experienced musher, for in the tent he had made himself a bed of fine spruce twigs which are warm and good to have under you, as the warmth of your body does not penetrate them and melt the snow beneath. The man was travelling alone, and he invited me to stay with him till day dawned, and to share his tent. I was glad to get out of more sledging in the dark, so with his help I unharnessed my dogs and then flung myself down by the fire, sharing his meal which happened to be just ready, and making myself snug on part of his bed of fragrant spruce-twigs.

We talked a bit about the trail and that sort of thing, for such talk comes easily and naturally to wayfarers, and I learned that he was heading for Fairbanks in order to get home as quickly as ever he could, home to Texas or Kentucky, or wherever it was— but it was a place where it was warm, so he told me, and not miserably cold as in that accursed Alaska.

Not that it had been too bad there, for the man had found gold; not so very much, yet enough for him to be able to buy a farm at home where he wouldn't freeze. And that was just what he was going to do, so that communicative man informed me; he hated Alaska to which he had gone just to try his luck and get the money for a farm as quickly as he could. And he had toiled and struggled and suffered for a couple of years or so, and done it.

Now that adventure was over and done with, now he was going home, He had a wife and six children—look here! And out of his pocket he produced a long and relatively clean white silk ribbon on which some artistic photographer had fixed prints of the family: that of his wife at the top, then below her the children in order of age. With a not too clean finger, he tenderly and carefully caressed the pictures on the silk and told me their names and what they were like, and what hopes he had for his kids, and how they would all get down to it when with his Alaska money he had bought that farm on which he had had his eye for so long.

He was a nice easy chap, more talkative than most you met on the trail, and when day dawned I requited his hospitality by inviting him to join up with me till we got to Fairbanks. I had good dogs and a fine sledge; he only three miserable creatures and an even more wretched sledge.

We travelled together for several days and thoroughly enjoyed each other's company, learning all about one another, and as well I learned about his wife and his children who were far better children than other people's. And he produced some crumpled letters, which had obviously been read over and over again in some smoke-filled hut, and read them out aloud with a far-away dreamy look in his eyes.

Then we reached the city, the centre of Alaska's second largest gold district, with its furious activity. Earth which had been mined out of deep shafts lay piled in huge heaps the size of small hills ready for washing when the warmth of spring had put the winter's cold to flight. The water to do the washing was obtained from some small rivers and from a large lake some thirty miles away, from which it was brought to those piles of earth in deep ditches and long pipe-lines. The shrill wails of factory hooters could be heard far out over the country, and though there were not so many men at work as usual in the district which for the second year had been stricken by strikes, there still seemed plenty of men. These were strike-breakers who hoped by toiling hard to get money enough to start up on their own and become big bosses like the men who each evening came and fetched the gold which had been washed and locked it away in great safes—yet that must have been a pretty vain hope considering the prices people had to pay there for the mere necessities of life, to say nothing of what it cost to add a little colour to existence.

The last bit of the trail into Fairbanks followed a railway line, and it was queer to see dog-teams and big horse sledges with jingling bells racing the clattering monster of a locomotive. And so we came into Fairbanks, a proper town and a big town, with everything which goes with that: hotels and restaurants, pubs as thick as flies on sugar, banks and electric light, engineering shops where they said they would make you anything up to and including a river-steamer. There were clubs and 'Moulins Rouges' galore, some quite big with room for a considerable number of people, others tiny, but one and all advertised in letters of flame *Danse intime*, whatever that meant. There was even a theatre in Fairbanks and several lecture halls which were mostly used for the big dinners the local bigwigs gave each other. And Fairbanks boasted no fewer than three newspapers, *Fairbanks Times* being said, by itself at least, to be the best in the country, and it was certainly the dearest, for it cost twenty-five cents a copy and consisted of just the one sheet of two printed pages.

There were shops in almost every building, big ones and fine ones, small ones and wretched ones, and also big department stores where everything was to be had at very high prices. There were pawnbrokers too, and they cheerfully sold the articles pawned with them for relatively little money, for they knew from experience that the poor devil who had been forced to pawn his possessions very seldom got the money to redeem them. And if he did happen to find gold, to strike rich, then the things he had pawned in his dire need seemed not worth bothering about in his unexpected prosperity, and he would buy new instead of redeeming the old.

There was an amazing number of jewellers' shops, whose glittering display of gold and pearls and precious stones drew the eyes of all the Fairbanks women. Other plate-glass windows also exhibited irresistible temptations in the shape of dresses and other articles of clothing which you would not otherwise see in Alaska and which, if you could rely on the printed word, were imported direct from Paris.

It was a fantastic thought that that large town with its ten thousand or so inhabitants was only six years old, and that it all rested on the uncertain foundation which gold after all is. Nobody, of course, had any idea how long the stream of gold would continue to flow, no one could be certain that the gold gained from that day's washings might not be the last. If that were the case Fairbanks would at once have been abandoned by every man and woman who could scrape together enough to buy a digger's outfit and go off to try their luck somewhere else in Alaska. The others would gradually sink into bitter poverty and either die or leave the country which had promised so much and given them so little.

Even the optimists who invested their every cent in Fairbanks, in land and buildings and such, realized that the town's future rested on the most fragile of foundations. The experts all prophesied that the town was doomed should the stream of gold ever dry, yet that was not what happened; when it did, Fairbanks went through a period of deep depression, but then it blossomed out again, and today is a university city of no mean size.

I don't suppose there was anyone there in 1908 with imagination enough to foresee that future; for in those days the fate of everything turned on gold, and the more clever diddled the less clever till he had to pawn his shirt without much hope of ever being able to redeem it.

None of that, however, affected me, and I did not give it a thought, as I and my friend from Kentucky turned away from the Tanana River one lovely spring morning with sparkling sunlight and glittering rime on the trees and drove jingling into the town to where some smiling men were standing waiting. They gave me a look and asked: 'Captain Mikkelsen?'

'Yes, sirs,' said I, and from that moment till I left I was one of the most favoured members of the community in that expensive town, able to taste any of the good things Fairbanks had to offer, to have whatever happened to take my fancy. Nome's telegram had even come as far as there, and of course a large rich town like Fairbanks could not possibly permit Nome to do more for me than it.

My Kentucky friend was brutally dismissed to fend for himself. I ventured a weak protest, but was told that he was only a digger, one of the small ones. The eye of experience had him summed up, after one appraising glance at his poor little outfit. Such small fry just didn't count, they explained ruthlessly.

I didn't like it, but the great ones of Fairbanks remained unmoved, and after I had said goodbye to the Kentucky man, wished him luck and good fortune with his farm and a speedy reunion with his family which I now felt I knew, my new friends dragged me off.

It was pleasant to be taken in hand by such hosts, and I enjoyed going about the big town with men who were known and who showed me all the sights and spoke with thinly veiled pride of the fabulous prices charged for everything in that Paris of the North, as the local patriots proudly called their town.

If they had wished to amaze me, they achieved their purpose, for the prices left me absolutely speechless. I had never imagined it possible that things could be so expensive as they were there, but the local patriots just laughed and said: 'We're so rich that price means nothing to us—nor to you either, friend Mikkelsen, we'll attend to that!'

That evening I was invited to a dinner in the town's largest club-house, so after I had washed and combed myself I put on my best suit of skins which I had mended and smartened up a bit as well as a man could, and off I went. When I got to the club I almost dropped with surprise: all the men were in evening dress, the women décolletée and hung with glittering jewellery, with spark-ling rings on their fingers, diamonds and gold everywhere where it could possibly be attached. The upper ten of Fairbanks were shamelessly parading their wealth, and it really was an impressive sight, which was what it was meant to be!

Naturally I was a little worried by my dress and became pro-gressively more so as the evening wore on and the heat in those expensively decorated rooms reached heights more suitable for those in thin dresses, than in skins. I felt as though I were in a Turkish bath. My kindly hosts regretted that they had not had time to conjure up evening dress for me, and told me just to remove my skin tunic. That unfortunately was just what I could not do. Those well meaning men no doubt had several dozen shirts at home, but I only possessed the one I had on, and had had on far longer than I liked to remember, so I just had to sit there sweating.

We ate and drank, drank hard, champagne at twenty or thirty dollars a bottle flowed like water. That sent our spirits up and loosened our tongues, and we talked of everything under the sun, including one subject of which they spoke cheerfully and expertly, though it was not a normal topic of conversation: treatment in prisons, which were the good ones where it wasn't so bad to be for a bit, and which it was best to keep out of.

I could not help hearing what they were saying, for they were all getting rather loud-voiced where I sat among the town's most eminent citizens. My astonishment must have been visible on my face, for a banker sitting beside me struck his glass for silence and said: 'Friends, don't talk so loud about prisons, remember our guest of honour, who is perhaps the only one of us who has not made personal acquaintance with one!'

There was a moment's amazed silence, then the babble broke out again, worse than ever, and I was none the wiser.

They were not boring people to be with, and I enjoyed the evening despite the heat and the talk of things of which I knew nothing—forgetting unfortunately a rather regrettable incident in Treport. They would certainly have been delighted if they thought they could have welcomed me into their company as a fully-qualified jail-bird!

When the elder members of the company were beginning to think of bed, some of the younger ones came up to me and said: 'When the old ones go home, we're going out to paint the town red. Will you come?'

I had no objection to that, and so we spent half the night doing the round of the restaurants and pubs, and not least of the '*danses intimes*,' and though I didn't dance, the others did, and we enjoyed ourselves as you do, or think you do, when you are young and slightly uplifted.

Those dance-halls were noisy places. The mechanical pianos thumped out tune after tune; the floors were usually crowded with dancing couples who all sang and laughed, shouted and shrieked. Drink flowed; here and there two tipsy men would quarrel over a girl and deal each other crashing blows for her favours. The electric light shone on barbarically gilded stucco on ceilings and walls, and mirrors which reached from floor to ceiling multiplied the billowing mass of humanity, an impression enough to make you feel giddy when you had been sledging alone for months on end.

That was life and those were merry days I spent in Fairbanks, where it seemed as though the whole town were celebrating, whether out on the streets, or in the many places of entertainment where experienced men and women diverted the gold from their customers' pockets to their own, a process which occasionally gave rise to a violent row with shrieks and bawls, police and all the rest of it.

In one such place I met my friend from Kentucky again. He was sitting on the floor in the corner of a large dance-hall. His eyes were melancholy, his hair was tousled, his mouth drooped and his clothes were torn. He was not enjoying himself any longer. Around him stood a little battery of empty and half-empty bottles, and the floor was awash with expensive wine. He had been making heavy weather of it.

When I arrived he had sobered up more or less, was sitting quietly and unnoticed in his corner, abandoned by all those who earlier that evening had drunk his health and been a grand help in emptying the bottles. He was fingering that silk ribbon with the photographs of his wife and six pretty children, clean no longer, and the tears were streaming down his cheeks. He gave me a melancholy smile when I asked him how he was.

'As you see,' he said and sighed, 'I had gold when I came here. Not much, but enough to buy that farm in Kentucky. And I was to have gone on with the post-sledge for Valdez tomorrow. Now, I've only this left'—and he held up the silk-ribbon for me to see. 'Can you get me a job with any of your rich friends? I am cleaned right out—and that farm in Kentucky has gone to the devil and the girls!'

That was that! It happened so often in Alaska. Sooner or later, on some cold winter's night, that man from Kentucky would find death and peace under a drift of snow beside some trail, and perhaps that was the best thing you could wish him—and those who waited for him in Kentucky.

CHAPTER XVIII

THE END OF THE ROAD

*I am transported like a VIP—The endless trail has an end after all—
The stranding of the* Saragossa—*A dilemma for a poor man—Moneyless
in Seattle—Home again*

My friends in Fairbanks would not hear of my leaving their city
in anything so antiquated as a sledge and dog-team. I was to drive
the last stretch of the road to Valdez as a personage of importance
behind galloping horses in the post-sledge; the city would take
care of that. So I said goodbye to my faithful dogs, gave them and
the sledge to the man from Kentucky, even though I felt fairly
certain that he would immediately convert them into spirits, and
taking my seat in the big post-sledge drove away from hospitable
Fairbanks.

That, of course, was an easy and very comfortable method of
travelling, but I didn't altogether like it. I no longer felt in tune
with Nature, as I had when driving with my own dog-team, when I
had been able to stop where I liked and do whatever entered my
head. But I must admit that I was tired of that everlasting mushing
and, even though it made me feel like a parcel which obliging
people had expressed at considerable expense so that it could get
to the coast as soon as possible, I enjoyed sitting in the big post-
sledge in my warm furs, gazing spellbound at the lovely scenery to
the west: jagged mountains with high snow-clad peaks standing
out sharply against the deep blue of the sky, as they shone in the
sunlight, and making a lovely sight above the dark-green of the
spruces, though they were perhaps even more beatuiful when we
drove across a stretch of tree-less country and could see the mighty
mountains towering directly out of the flat plain.

I felt slightly ashamed. There was I, for no merit of my own,
driving like a great personage in a comfortable sledge behind a
team of four horses which took us thundering down the trail at
twenty miles an hour, thrusting road-weary wayfarers off into the

deep snow at the side. Most of those were fagged-out, desperate, poor deluded devils who had walked the three, four hundred miles from Valdez, inadequately clad, freezing and hungry, their feet knocked up, their boots worn out, most of them indeed in old rubber-boots which were the worst imaginable footgear for cold. They stood in groups outside the many roadhouses along the trail, listening to the laughter and singing within and inhaling the delicious smells of cooking they could not afford to sample while taking their ease in the company of happier men. They were mostly strike-breakers, six hundred of whom were laboriously on the long march from Valdez to the gold district where the strike had just been called off and where there was already more labour than was wanted. What, I wondered, would happen to them when they eventually reached Fairbanks, where rumour and unscrupulous agents had persuaded them they would be able to earn princely wages for little work.

Storms came, such storms that even the great post-sledge swung about like a ship in a heavy sea, slithering across the smooth hard track and coming dangerously near the deep ravines alongside. The weather became so bad that we had to stop at a post-house, where most of the passengers were transferred into other one-horse sledges, where you snuggled down into warm hay and were snugly tucked up in elk-skins by friendly ostlers, and so drove on, each horse meekly following the next.

That, however, was too much for me, and I protested loudly. To be coddled like that was well enough for those who were not accustomed to the hardships of the sledge-trail, for soft men and pampered women; but for one who had sledged all those thousands of miles, it was humiliating and degrading.

The storms, however, could become so severe and the snow so deep that even we who were left in the post-sledge had to halt and wait for the weather to improve. For two days and nights we were stormbound in a roadhouse called 'Our Home' which was filled to capacity before we arrived, yet hospitably opened its doors to all travellers from north or south who could not get farther because of the storm and snow. In the end there were eighteen of us in that little hut, including five women, and all day long we men sat round a red-hot stove, smoking bad tobacco and telling those newly arrived from the south tales of the horrors of the trail. It must have been edifying talk for people who did not know the country, or realize that exaggeration often had to take the place of truth, when men had been so long in each other's company that they had exhausted all topics of conversation that women might hear.

Apparently we went too far, for one of the women became hysterical and began to weep convulsively, wanting to go back home to the States, and to comfort her we had to eat all our words and swear that our stories had been all lies and invention. But that too was a lie, the worst of all—for most of what we had told had had more than a grain of truth in it.

At night we all slept in the same room, the men two and two in narrow bunks, the women withdrawn modestly behind a threadbare rug. We were all glad when the weather improved so that we could get on our way. And the scared woman went north after all. She had a long way to go, so sooner or later she must have discovered that after all our tales of sledging in Alaska had been nearer the truth than not.

It was then the end of March. The equinox lay behind us, and the spring was at hand. The sun was shining, and the forty degrees of frost felt like a foretaste of summer. Every single twig in the great forest was covered with rime which glistened in the sunlight, and against the gay blue of the sky we could see the gleaming ice-peak of Wrangel volcano, looking quite close, but in reality over forty miles away. From its top billowed a cloud of smoke which gleamed yellow in the sunlight—a lovely sight which aroused in me longings for something I had seen as a young sailor and been fascinated by: the untrodden mountains in the interior of New Guinea.

We drove hard and long in order to make up for lost time. As the daylight ebbed and a full moon rose up to light us, we drove through a town of tents erected by the men of the convoy, which was taking the great quantities of goods landed by the steamer at Valdez to the shops in Fairbanks and Fort Gibbon's store of telephone equipment. It all had to be got there before the warmth of the early summer put an end to sledging, and thus to all transport of goods into the interior.

In that still, clear frosty weather we could hear the deep hum of the men's voices, their singing and the shrill notes of a mouth organ while we were still quite a long way off. Then we drove into that town where the tents stood in long rows on either side of the track. Lanterns burned in them all so that they glowed in the night, and as we swept down the long street of tents, its exuberant inhabitants came running out cracking whips, urging on the horses, calling out to us, the homeward bound. Beside every tent stood horses munching oats, and yet so cold that they shook in spite of the warm rugs they all had spread over them.

We were afraid that such a large convoy must have knocked the trail to pieces, and no sooner were we through the 'town' of tents than our fears became bitter certainty. From that moment till we reached Valdez the sledge never stopped dropping into deep holes worn in the trail by the heavy goods sledges, and it swung to and fro and pitched on the snow like a ship in a storm. But we had to push on, and push on we did, crawling laboriously up the steep mountain slopes to the pass high above our heads, from which we would be able to see the endless expanse of the Pacific if the weather were good.

But it wasn't. We did the last fifteen miles of my nearly 3,000 mile journey through Alaska in storm and snow with a double team, and even then the horses had a hard job of it. We could scarcely see three or four sledge-lengths ahead of us, and the trail was narrow, carved out of the cliff with a perpendicular drop of 1,000 feet to the bottom of Keystone Canyon on the one side, which was uncomfortable enough when the sledge skidded across the trail like a rudderless ship on a stormy sea—with the passengers standing up in it ready to jump if it went over the edge.

Things went all right, and we got through the dreaded canyon which, according to old Indian legend, is supposed to be the abode of a dreadfully evil spirit which requires a human sacrifice every day and which gives birth to all the raging storms that harry the Valdez area—and they are many.

Just beyond the southern end of the canyon we came to a town with roadhouses and big guest-tents crowding together, then to a railway track some optimists had started building and hoped to be able to continue through the pass sometime in the future, and which they did in fact get built after many abortive attempts. From there our way was marked with rusty iron, light railway track and all sorts of old junk; and everywhere were half-finished houses, the wind howling and shrieking in and out of their window openings and the rectangular holes where doors would be put if they ever could afford to get the houses finished, that is to say, if the stream of gold at Fairbanks continued to flow. If not, then everything there would be lost. There were sledges laden with goods for the interior, also a last remnant of the melancholy army of the strike-breakers, then a last bend, and there just ahead of us lay the Pacific, black and unending, and by the coast a little town which was Valdez, and by the quay a steamer with smoke pouring from the funnel and a Blue Peter at the fore-top. It was high time we arrived, for there would not be another steamer going south for a month.

We all wanted to catch the steamer, so the driver cracked his long whip above his steaming horses' heads and we thundered through the streets of the little town sweeping pedestrians aside like a troop of charging cavalry, while we passengers stood up in the sledge and shouted and called our own encouragements to the horses.

We reached the steamer just as she was going to take in her moorings, drove up alongside the great black hull, seized our baggage including my kitbag with the damned gold which was still there in spite of everything; willing hands helped us heave it all aboard, and with a farewell bellow the steamer moved out from the quay, and I heaved a great sigh of relief—six months all but seven days my sledge trip had taken; I had begun it as an act of defiance and often regretted that I had, but now it was over, and I had a wealth of glorious memories from it.

The steamer was called *Saragossa*. She was a passenger ship built for the run between New York and the West Indies and had once been a lovely vessel, but now she was old and worn, though still good enough to sail the dangerous Alaskan coast where so much might happen. Later I was to discover that that was exactly what the owners had thought, which was why they had only insured her against total loss. There were so many reefs and rocks in those waters that sooner or later the ship was bound to run on one of them, and whether charted or uncharted was a matter of indifference from their point of view, provided they got the large sum for which the steamer was insured.

We put in at some small harbours further down the coast, and the skipper, Kragh his name was, and I soon became firm friends, for we were both sailors, and, as he was a Norwegian, we were in a way fellow-countrymen as well.

I suppose I must have boasted a bit about my sledge journey and that may have irritated Kragh the Norwegian, who thought that only Norwegians could sledge over land and sea, for when we were due to put out from our last port of call—I happened to be up on the bridge with him—he turned to me and said with a wry smile: 'Yes, boy, you can sledge and I can't; but perhaps I can man-oeuvre my ship better than you—and I know the channels here like my own trousers' pocket.'

Now I had never doubted, let alone contested that, quite the contrary, but perhaps I had not admired him sufficiently and also talked a bit too much about what I could do, so that now he felt he would show off a bit.

'You watch,' Kragh went on, 'when we go out from here I'll let all the moorings go at the same time and ring up full speed ahead. You stand here with your watch in your hand and when fourteen minutes have passed you say "Ready," and exactly fifteen minutes after I've rung full speed, you say "Stop," then I'll put the helm hard over to starboard, and if you care to look over the starboard side you will see a large submerged rock four or five fathoms away, perhaps only three.'

'Fine,' said I, 'You certainly know your channels, skipper. I'm ready. Go ahead when you like.'

Then the orders rang out: Cast off fore and aft, and, when the hawsers were hauled in, the machine telegraph rang. The screw began to churn up the water at the stern, the ship gathered speed, more and more, shooting ahead, while I counted the minutes: I looked at Kragh, now—'Ready!' And a minute later: 'Stop!'

'Hard to starboard!' Kragh called to the helmsman, who spun the wheel hard over; and while the skipper stood by the machine-telegraph looking triumphant I ran towards the rail to see that submerged rock by the ship's side. But I never got so far before there was a crunching, grating sound; the ship quivered, cocked her bows up high, dropped her stern a bit—and there she sat, immovable.

The rock was there, that was quite certain; only the ship had gone three or four fathoms too far to starboard. She was right on it!

The machine-telegraph clanged, agitated orders rang out across the ship, the passengers rushed panic-stricken on deck, and I stole softly down from the bridge: at moments of disaster the man with responsibility is best left alone. And what could I have said to my friend Kragh? That it was a pity it had happened, or what? Words to comfort are not easily found in a situation like that. I preferred to say nothing and vanish.

It was not long before all on board realized that the tide was going out and that the situation was grave—for the ship, though not for us. The weather was relatively good, and we were not far from land.

The ship heeled over more and more as the water fell, and all the landlubbers on board got into a panic. The women shrieked, the men put on their lifebelts and looked very grave, and cursed till the sparks flew—and altogether without reason, for when the tide was right out cows could graze along *Saragossa*'s rusty sides.

The weather was beginning to look a bit threatening. The wind had got up a bit and small choppy seas began to show their teeth round the rock and *Saragossa's* stern. Black clouds came up and blotted out the mountains on land; there was snow in the air, perhaps dirty weather, and Kragh sent for me: 'Things didn't go quite as I had expected. I was a bit rash, I suppose—and too sure of myself,' he added with a sigh. For a moment he stood looking at the rock and the ship, and then went on: 'At high water I'll perhaps get her floated off; she struck on the ebb. We'll have a lot to do and I must keep the whole crew on board, but I would like to be rid of this shrieking hysterical mob of passengers. They're only in the way, and the weather doesn't look too reliable either. The passengers must leave the ship. Will you take them ashore in the lifeboats? But you can only have the catering staff to row; I can't spare any of the rest of the crew.'

'Yes, skipper,' I replied, glad to be of some use, and shortly afterwards the boats lay alongside. The passengers came up dragging their goods and gear and wanting to take it all with them, but they could only be allowed the most essential, and in rising wind and seas I set off with my six boats. It was not easy to get the stewards and male passengers to take to the oars, but a heavy tiller has considerable powers of persuasion, and, remembering a few of the words the Spaniard had used to get my dogs to pull extra hard, I used them then, also with good results.

Taking it all in all it didn't go so badly. The women wailed and thought we should all drown; while the men rowed and cursed angrily at having had to leave most of their possessions on board; nor was that so strange, for their baggage must have held all the gold and the money they had toiled so hard to get. The Nome shopkeeper's gold was in the same predicament, for my kitbag had been left on board with the rest, but I didn't give that many thoughts.

The stranding had been seen from the shore, and when we had been rowing about an hour, a little coasting steamer came out, took us in tow and brought us to land, where all but the bedridden had assembled at the jetty to receive us and ask: how—and why?

I was, I suppose, the only sailor in the town other than the skipper of the little coastal steamer which had towed us in, and the sheriff appointed us both surveyors to decide whether the ship could be salvaged or not. For the first time in its history that little town on the Alaskan coast attracted a lot of attention in America. The telegraph wire hummed as telegrams flew to and fro, and shortly after I was appointed surveyor I received one from *Saragossa's* owners telling me in veiled language that if *Saragossa* became a total loss all my expenses would be covered by the owners no matter how large. Shortly afterwards I received another telegram, this time from the underwriters who wished to have the ship salvaged at any price. And money was absolutely of no consequence, I could take whatever steps I liked.

All this talk of money sounded a bit mysterious. I didn't really see what they were driving at.

As surveyor I had to go aboard *Saragossa* again, and there I had a talk with Kragh, who knew conditions on the Pacific coast much better than I and could interpret the telegram for me.

'You see,' he said, 'the ship is only insured against total loss, and if she floats off, the underwriters won't have to pay anything. You could then go up to their offices when you get to Seattle, and tell them that you were surveyor and said: the ship had to be salvaged, and she was salvaged—but that it was expensive. Presumably you would then get a fat cheque for your trouble. But if the ship remained perched on this rock, you can go to the owners and tell them that you as impartial surveyor considered that it was quite out of the question to salvage the ship and that she had to be condemned. And presumably you will also be given a cheque. The telegram almost says as much.

'Now you can choose which you want,' Kragh went on. 'There's a bit of rascality in either. But that's normal on the coast here. Whatever happens, you can make a nice bit out of this wreck— but I get the kick. I'm finished as a skipper!'

It was a painful situation to have got into for no fault of one's own, apart from a little innocent boasting. The sheriff was also on board, as was the other surveyor who presumably had similar telegrams in his pocket, and he looked a bit horrified and disconcerted when I demanded a meeting in the presence of the representative of the law, and there before witnesses asked to be relieved of the duty of surveyor. The sheriff could not understand that and talked a lot about money. Perhaps he too had received similar mysterious telegrams; but I insisted and demanded that it would be put on record that I renounced the job. He gave way in the end, and I felt a bit of a saint, when I saw my refusal written down in his official protocol, because I knew very well that I should not have a cent in my pocket when I eventually reached Seattle, where I could scarcely expect to be given a bag of gold as I had in Alaska, but all the same—my future peace of mind was no doubt worth the money which I could perhaps have got from owners or underwriters whether the matter was decided in favour of one side or the other.

Saragossa decided the issue herself three days after she stranded by breaking in two amidships, so that even a blind man could have told you that that ship would never sail the Pacific again.

The passengers' belongings were taken ashore before *Saragossa* broke in two, and joyful and noisy were the reunions. When each had got his, the recovery had to be celebrated in the pubs. I was rather annoyed, for my kitbag with the shopkeeper's gold was also brought ashore, and though I may have deserved that, he certainly had not. But that's how it is.

We had to wait a whole month in that dreadful hole before another steamer came and took us on board, and by that time *Saragossa* had already been pounded to pieces by the huge waves and seas of the Pacific. And as we passed the rock at a respectful distance, Kragh came up to me and said: 'I'm relying on you, you won't say anything?'

And I haven't—until now.

A couple of weeks later we tied up in Seattle harbour. On the quay was a crowd of people come to meet the shipwrecked and whoever else might have arrived from the fabulous land of gold. Among them was a man whose voice rose above the confused hum of arrival in continual shouts of 'Is Mikkelsen on board?'

I heard him all right, and I recognized him by his description as the Nome shopkeeper's partner. I knew too why he was so interested in whether or not I was on board, but I liked neither his appearance nor his insistence, and I thought it would do him good to sweat with anxiety for a while, as I had sweated lugging his gold about. So I hid behind all the other passengers and paid no attention to his increasingly apprehensive cries. However, he could not be kept in ignorance very long, and when I eventually went ashore with my far-travelled kitbag, he fell upon me on the gangway with the question: 'Have you got the gold? Where is it?'

We unpacked it in a shed on the quay, and he counted the bags weighed them in his hand as if to feel whether they were roughly the same weight as those I had been given in Nome, and with a nod to me he prepared to go with his treasure.

'Yes, that's the lot,' said I, rather peeved at the man's obvious suspicion, 'The devil take all your gold, as I hope he will also take you. Just carting the muck about has cost me buckets of sweat and endangered my soul because of all the oaths and curses I have expended on it. So it seems to me—!'

But I got no further; the jocular hint was wasted on him, or else he did not want to understand it. He said nothing, just put the gold into a suitcase he had brought with him, and with a curt nod of farewell he disappeared into the crowd. Naturally, I never saw him again, and a good thing too; but there I stood in the shed with my kitbag, so much lighter now, and the sack with my papers; but I had no money whatever and I did not feel very cheerful. And then I had to answer all the questions inquisitive journalists had to ask about the land in the pack-ice north of Alaska, about my long journey by sledge, the loss of the *Saragossa*, and lots more.

It was all pretty unpleasant, for to be without money in a strange town is certainly not a nice feeling. However, I did have one friend in Seattle, a Danish miller, called Lehmann, who had helped me a lot before, and it was for his house that I now set course. There I got a lunch I badly needed and kindness and understanding from him, his wife and his happy children who had no idea of life's difficulties.

It was like coming home again and I revelled in it—but I did not feel very jaunty when I had to tell Lehmann that I was absolutely penniless and ask him if he would lend me the bare minimum which I would repay when—when?

How the good Lehmann laughed: 'You've been penniless before," he said, 'and undoubtedly will be again. I'm sure you're a bad debtor, but even so, what you need you can borrow from me.'

So that difficulty was surmounted, and shortly afterwards I was hurtling eastwards along the singing rails to New York. A very short stay there, and then I was on Danish soil again as passenger in *Oscar II* which brought me to Copenhagen and so home to my parents' house.

My poor parents had had another fright on top of the telegram from Dawson City, when the American and Danish newspapers printed drastic descriptions of the appalling wreck of the *Saragossa* off the snow-clad coast of Alaska, which were accompanied by horrifying drawings of the crew and poor passengers lashed to the rigging, while the storm whipped huge seas over the doomed vessel and snow swirled so thick that you could scarcely see what was what. Lies and invention the whole of it, like so much else you could read in the papers.

The newspapers had also reported what unfortunately was only too true, that I had not found the undiscovered land north of Alaska, but some peculiar thing of no interest to anybody: the edge of the Continental shelf. What could you do with that?

And at that time I had no suspicion that there were those huge floating islands of ice they long afterwards found in the Beaufort Sea—and from my point of view that was a pity.

CHAPTER XIX

FORTY YEARS ON

Vain attempt to start a new Expedition—Thoughts during a flight across the Davis Straits—A startling telegram—Discovery of 'something' in the Beaufort Sea—The floating ice-islands—Aeroplanes land on an aircraft carrier of ice—The Americans build a meteorological station there—So there was something in the Beaufort Sea

IT is so long now since I started that expedition to Alaska that I no longer remember the details exactly, and it is possible, perhaps even probable, that in order to get money to search for the unknown land in the Beaufort Sea I had beaten the big drum a bit too hard, and perhaps also been too self-assured in asserting its existence. For when I got home from the expedition, it was obvious, even to me, that none of my friends really believed that I was going to be satisfied with having toiled across the pack-ice out over the deep Arctic Ocean merely to ascertain that the land did not exist. And to a certain extent they were right. Naturally, I would rather have found the land than the edge of the Continental shelf, but I could not conjure up land where land was not, so willy-nilly I had to be satisfied with the negative result of my search and patiently accept my friends' somewhat sarcastic questions about what the land in the wilderness of ice looked like.

I did not in any way feel defeated by my failure, for even before I got back to civilization after my sledge journey to the south, I had decided in my own mind that I would make another attempt to equip an expedition into the Beaufort Sea which I now knew so much better. And I was still convinced that land, or some other obstacle to the normal drift of the ice, must exist somewhere or other in that huge area of sea between the north coast of America the Canadian islands, and the Pole.

But where was I to find the money which such an expedition would cost? It had been hard enough the first time, and that was a small amount compared to what I now considered necessary.

204

Optimistically I put the amount at some 300,000 Danish Crowns, perhaps 400,000. That was a lot of money, and I had been well aware from the moment I began sledging homewards from Flaxman Island, that it would probably prove difficult to raise. But without a lot of money there could be no new expedition.

I was absolutely penniless when I reached Copenhagen. In actual fact it was worse than that, for I had shamelessly exploited my credit to the uttermost merely to enable myself to get started those two years ago. And then, too, I had given bonds for quite considerable sums right and left, both before I set out and after I returned to civilized parts and ordered society, where it was absolutely essential to have money in order to exist and where people regarded it with the deepest respect and seemed to judge a man's ability and knowledge by the smaller or larger extent of the bank balance they thought they could glimpse behind him.

Thus, in spite of everything, I found life easier to live in uncivilized Alaska with its hard-boiled population, where most people just collected money as a sport and for the fun of being able to squander it with both hands when the time for playing the fool came and they had nothing else to think about. That was an attitude I could understand and appreciate, but it was perhaps a dangerous one to acquire.

I certainly did not expect to find people in Denmark willing to give money for a new expedition to Alaska, but I hoped that I should again be able to find sympathy in England, and when, shortly after my return, the Royal Geographical Society invited me to give a lecture about the expedition in London, I took it as a lucky omen and a sign that perhaps I should once more succeed in finding there men to hazard large sums of money to enable one more blank spot to be filled in on the map of the world.

As I left Denmark to go to London, I felt almost certain that I would. On this occasion I wasn't nearly so anxious or confused as when I had mounted the rostrum in the RGS to tell my audience what I hoped I should find in the Beaufort Sea—and how. I now considered that I had mastered the language pretty well, and when I ended my lecture, I for one thought I had managed it pretty well—a bit long perhaps, but I had kept my eye the whole time on a rather somnolent-looking individual in one of the front rows and as he had not fallen asleep, I took that as a very favourable sign.

Naturally I was very interested to see what the newspapers had to say about my lecture. As I read them I felt more and more pleased; but one left me with a slightly bitter taste in my mouth by writing: 'Mr Mikkelsen spoke most beautiful American!'

I suppose that was not to be wondered at considering that for the last couple of years I had only been with Americans, but my vanity suffered a bit, as I had thought I spoke English.

What was bad, though, was the fact that although the RGS again promised me its moral and financial support for another expedition, I very soon realized that it was going to be more than difficult to raise the money for it—even in England. The Duchess of Bedford was no longer interested, and I had acquired sufficient worldly wisdom not to rely on getting money in America as it was needed. I had not forgotten the lesson that banker in Victoria had given me when he said: 'It came off, skipper, but it shouldn't have'—with a lot of emphasis on 'shouldn't.'

That remark kept chafing at my mind and, then as later, induced in me a certain caution in money matters.

In the end, after months of effort, I had to admit that it was not going to be possible to get the 400,000 crowns or so necessary for a new Alaskan Expedition. My previous experience in America was not such as to encourage me either: the millionaires there were surrounded by far too many zealous men whose duty it was to protect them and keep fanatics at a respectful distance from their money bags.

Perhaps, too, my enthusiasm was not quite so ardent as on the first occasion. The hardships of the pack-ice and of the journey back had perhaps cooled it a bit after all. Then too I was a few years older and perhaps age had made me a bit more sensible about money. Anyway, to make a long and a sad story short, after some months' vain hunting, I had to admit even to myself that I was not going to get the money either in Denmark, England or America, and whether I liked it or not I should have to put up with the idea that in the years to come someone else perhaps would be lucky enough to find the land to the north of Alaska.

In the quiet hours which come on occasion to even the most rest-less soul, and in which he reviews his passage so far across the stormy sea of life, I have often had to admit to myself that the Alaskan Expedition was very far from yielding the results which I had hoped for and expected, and which others had also expected.

I had not found the unknown land, but I still believed in it, and after my return from Alaska I fought hard to defend my conviction that somewhere or other in the Beaufort Sea there must be land to bind the drifting ice so that it became palaeocrystic, the age-old ice with hills and valleys, rivers and plains, just like proper land, across which we had sledged in 1907.

My friends were inclined to be sarcastic, told me that I had always been a fantast, and it was only too obvious that they did not believe in the existence of land up there in the vicinity of the North Pole. Those who were not friends, and you inevitably acquire some of those as the years go by, thought and said the same thing, though in far less gentle terms.

All that did not shake my belief that I was right and that one day the proof would be found. How often did I not stand bent over a map of the huge area between the north coast of America, the big Canadian Islands and the North Pole, wishing that it were not a piece of paper I was looking at but the earth itself which somehow or other I was viewing from somewhere up in space. That surely would have enabled me to see things which would have answered the many 'whys' over which I had puzzled ever since I first heard of the Beaufort Sea: why were ice-conditions there as peculiar as we had found them to be? Why were tides and currents as they were? What was it that had made the crews of the early whalers say that they had seen land out from Camden Bay? Why had even experienced and reliable men in an English man-of-war said the same in the 'seventies? Why should those men lie? What object could they possibly have had?

In the years afterwards while I was sledging and sailing across other lands and seas than Alaska and the Arctic Ocean, I never gave up hope that others would be luckier than I, and find that land, and so prove me right and wipe the bitterness of defeat from my mind. But, the decades passed without anyone apparently coming any nearer the solution of the mystery.

One of the many things which have happened in the world since 1906 is that the invention of the aeroplane has made the age-old laborious method of travelling in polar regions by sledge and dog-team hopelessly antiquated. One day in the spring of 1945 I, who have lived life to the full and made use of every opportunity to travel to places where the world and his wife do not go, found myself standing on an airfield in south-west Greenland looking admiringly at a four-engined 'plane which was to take me and a score of others across the sea to Labrador. It was the first time I had had a chance to fly over ice-covered sea, and I was very interested to see how it would look from a vantage point so high that you felt you had strayed in among the nebulae of the Milky Way.

The engines started with a great roar and commotion, and amid clouds of swirling snow churned up by the propellers we taxied across an airfield which technique and complete disregard for expense had created in what had been trackless unknown country a few decades ago, then the 'plane swung high across the encircling mountains with their glistening caps of ice and headed westwards across the ice-filled sea.

Sitting there comfortably in an upholstered armchair in an electrically heated cabin, I gazed spellbound at the pack-ice in Davis Strait some four miles below me, and at the coast of Greenland stretching for hundreds of miles to the north. Then I remembered my sledge journey across the ice of the Beaufort Sea in 1907, and thought of the land I had been trying to find and of the mysteries hidden in that ice-covered sea; I remembered too with a smile the labour it had been in those old days to get dogs and sledges across the pack-ice, while the aeroplane in which I now sat could fly in an hour or two the distance it would have taken me fifty days' sledging to cover in those days of antiquity in transport. From such a height too it must be possible to see enormous distances, and I realized that now the old problems could be solved without great difficulty and that at last I might expect it to be settled whether I or the sceptics were right.

That happened even quicker than I had expected.

The second world war was hardly at an end before the air above the Beaufort Sea became almost crowded with huge aeroplanes roaring across it from the airfields of Alaska on routine flights to the Pole. Then one morning in 1950 I opened my newspaper and, after glancing at the headlines to learn the worst, I happened to see tucked away in a corner an item of news of interest to scarcely anyone in the world but to me and a handful of Arctic experts.

It was a cable from America reporting briefly how young Colonel Joseph O. Fletcher on a routine flight to the Pole in August 1946 had seen something remarkable on his radar screen as he flew across the Beaufort Sea at a great height, but whether it were land or some huge extraordinary ice formation he had not been able to determine.

So, there was 'something' in the Beaufort Sea after all—and thus my expedition of 1906-08 had not been quite so stupid as some people had tried to make out. That was good to know.

It quickly transpired that it was definitely not land they had discovered in the Beaufort Sea; what was there and which looked like land and at the beginning had been taken for land, shifted position noticeably, and most Arctic experts regarded Joe Fletcher's 'something' as more sensational than the discovery of an island would have been.

The 'something' was sighted some 270 miles north-north-east of Point Barrow. At first it was kept a deep military secret and was put under observation. Soon, however, it was realized that it must be an ice-floe of quite fantastic dimensions. It was measured and pronounced to have an area of 520 square kilometres. At first the initiated called it a 'floating island,' but that was eventually changed to 'floating ice-island,' and as such it will go into Arctic literature as one of the great and significant discoveries in the Arctic Ocean.

These ice-islands drifted with the current, slowly and sedately, almost imperceptibly, yet in the weeks, months and years moving quite considerable distances. The first ice-island to be observed drifted some fifteen hundred miles in a full three years, and the Arctic experts were very busy trying to discover how it came into being, whence it had come and where it would drift.

When the weather was good with the sun shining and no wind, the great aeroplanes would roar off taking scientists to study the appearance and structure of the ice-islands from as close quarters as they could get. Their descriptions of the ice-islands' appearance and surface corresponded exactly to the ice we had seen and sledged across in 1907: rounded hills with wide valleys between, seen from the distance and in the right light, a ghost land, land so far away that only its highest peaks could be seen above the horizon of ice like mountains blue with distance.

It was undoubtedly ice of the same kind which the whalers and crew of *Plover* had seen in the Beaufort Sea and thought to be undiscovered land. It must have been ice of that kind which the sharp-eyed Eskimoes had so often seen to the north and thought to be land, and which imagination and legend had turned into a hunter's paradise in the wilderness of ice, the abode of their ideal beauties, women obese and bursting.

And it must have been detached pieces of these enormous ice-floes which we had so confidently sledged across in our search for land in 1907, not large like the largest ice-islands they had now discovered—for then we certainly would have thought it was land and would have announced our discovery of it—but large enough to make us wonder. But we had had no suspicion of the connection between them and the land we sought, nor any idea that what we had seen was the natural phenomenon now called a 'floating ice-island.'

Our estimate of what would have awaited us if we had drifted past Point Barrow was quite correct: we must have met our death somewhere in the mighty Arctic Ocean; for it was discovered after several years' aerial observation of these ice-islands that they came from the north coast of Ellesmere Land, drifted southwards along the big Canadian islands and so across the Beaufort Sea near Alaska and very near where we had been with our sledges in 1907. Off Point Barrow they turn north and continue at a speed of a couple of miles or so in the twenty-four hours towards the North Pole and at the time of writing, in 1954, are on their way back towards the Beaufort Sea. Thus if we had not reached land when we did those forty-six years ago, somewhere about the year 1910, our ice-island would have drifted over or very near to the North Pole carrying on its hilly surface the frozen remains of three rash young men.

When they had thoroughly examined those ice-islands from the air, photographed them from every angle, mapped them like true land, watched them for a few years so that they were recognizable by certain characteristic formations and people knew where to find them at any given moment, they began to wonder whether it wouldn't be possible to find a flat area sufficiently large to land an aeroplane on.

A suitable one was found, and on 19 March 1952, Colonel Joseph O. Fletcher landed his big Dakota on the huge ice-island some 130 miles from the Pole, while three Skymasters circled overhead keeping the world informed of what was happening. It was a bold undertaking, and after one or two attempts they brought it off. A few days later I read this about it in my newspaper:

'After the Dakota had landed photographer George Silk crawled out of the 'plane to take some photographs. General Old . . . walked in 97 degrees of frost along the track in the ice made by the 'plane in landing, and when he got back to the Dakota, he said to Fletcher: "I cannot see how any human being could support life here." The two remained talking in low voices together, standing only a few inches apart, and they shielded their faces with their hands from the cold which was so great that it paralysed the men's words and thoughts. Now and then they took their hands from their faces and jumped about violently to get a little warmth into their bodies, talking all the while. In the end General Old gave Fletcher the permission he wanted for him and his two men to stay on the ice, and everybody turned to unloading the equipment.'

Life's photographer George Silk maintained that it was so cold on the ice-island that they could not work quickly, a piece of information most surprising to an old Arctic hand who had always thought that you could get yourself more or less warm by working. And as, according to Silk, it wasn't possible to think clearly in that appalling cold, one can only wonder at the good photographs he took of the first thing the men did on the ice-island which was to build an igloo and also of the ceremony when General Old planted the American flag in the ice and proclaimed the ice-island an American area which he named after the man who was the first to have seen it and landed on it: Joseph O. Fletcher.

Then the big Dakota took off in a cloud of swirling snow and, followed by its three Skymasters, flew southwards to Alaska and warmer climes where thought was not paralysed by the cold, leaving on the ice the three men who had volunteered to spend a year or so on the ice-island.

Fletcher and his two companions knew exactly what they wanted. They at once set about making the island habitable, building some igloos, erecting a little town of tents near the landing place, and started sending weather reports to Thule. Fletcher's initiative had given America an aircraft-carrier of huge dimensions right in the middle of the Arctic Ocean, and she had thereby been able to stop a gap in the chain of meteorological stations and receive weather reports of the utmost value from a place in the Arctic from which until then it had not been possible to obtain information.

In the months that followed a succession of great 'planes roared

The American station on Fletcher Island, December 1952.

Colonel Joseph D. Fletcher after the landing on Fletcher Island.

hotographed by the light of a full moon by Herbert Davsey.

The ice-island 'T3,' Fletcher Island, photographed at 13,000 feet and from a distance of about a hundred miles.

out from an aerodrome well within Alaska across the melancholy
tundra and over the Beaufort Sea to Fletcher Island, which was
drifting along sedately with the current less than two hundred
miles from the Pole. When the 'planes reached the island a trap
in their bellies opened and in a minute a whole cargo was tumbled
out into the air which filled with coloured parachutes carrying
building material, instruments, fuel, everything, to the three men
on the ice, who were to be as comfortable and as well cared for as
a great nation could make them.

To make it easier and less risky to land supplies it was decided
to construct a landing ground for big transport 'planes on the ice.
As this could not all be done by hand, they dropped a bulldozer
and with that levelled ice hills, filled in holes and smoothed a mile
or so of runway. Then after the necessary marking and signalling
equipment had been dropped the landing ground was ready, and
Fletcher Island reported itself prepared to accept 'planes and to
build a meteorological station.

Men and material were landed and a meteorological station built
on that enormous ice-floe which has been found to be between 100
and 120 feet thick and which is calculated to contain about seven
milliard tons of ice. This enormous aircraft carrier drifts along
quite unaffected by what man does on it, and there live a dozen
or so men who have absolutely everything they could possibly
require and are never out of touch by wireless with the outside
world.

Those who work there must scarcely notice that they are living
only a hundred miles or so from the North Pole, and you hear no
more about the dreadful cold being able to numb people's thoughts
and ability to work. The first little igloos and nylon tents have been
replaced by proper houses with central heating, baths and all the
rest of it, all brought by air the long way from Alaska and farther.
An entire electric plant has been flown out, so that the people
there can live during the five months of night in houses which have
proper lights and have current all the year round for their wireless
transmitters, echo-sounders and the huge radar scanner mounted

there which will tell them despite fog or darkness if anyone is approaching that outpost of America.

They have also built a complete engineering workshop on Fletcher Island and have the mechanics to repair any of the instruments or machinery which may break down. So good are the facilities that one 'plane which had an engine break down over the Pole landed comfortably on Fletcher Island to have the engine changed.

A fresh engine was flown up to Fletcher Island and installed in the 'plane by the mechanics there and after a few weeks spent near the Pole the 'plane took off again and flew on its way as though nothing had happened.

'Planes often take off from the polar aircraft carrier to perform some scientific duty over the Pole, and when they are finished they fly back to their base, which drifts through the long golden days of summer and the equally long dark stormy winter as winds and currents decree, but all the time outside those parts to which previously Polar expeditions had been able to reach. Joe Fletcher's discovery of the ice-island in 1946 and America's taking possession of it in 1952 have started a new chapter in the great story of Polar research.

Recently I had a letter from a friend who had just paid a visit to the north coast of Alaska telling me of great building activity at a place on that desolate coast where they were intending to make a harbour and especially an airfield, where 'planes will be able to take off and land as they journey to and fro across the Arctic Ocean. This place was not far from where we wintered with *Duchess of Bedford* and it is now marked on the latest official map as Mikkelsen's Bay.

It is nearly half a century since I was on the coast of Alaska and, after wintering some sixty miles from this new harbour and airfield, sledged off across the pack-ice in search of the unknown land in the Beaufort Sea. It wasn't there, though there was 'something' which would have been well worth our efforts if we had had any idea that what we were sledging across were pieces of gigantic ice-floes, fantastically thick, with hills and valleys, gravel and stones, and most deceptively like land.

Now we know better. It was not land, but it may have been pieces of the 'floating ice-islands' which were discovered many years later from high-flying 'planes and which could never have been discovered without the aeroplane.

Presumably for many years to come there will be a constant stream of aeroplanes leaving the north coast of Alaska for Fletcher Island and the big military airfield at Thule, or for the North Pole, and it is to be hoped that as many will come back as go out. It is not impossible that some of these 'planes, on their outward or homeward flight, will land on the airfield which bears my name.

It is, too, possible that some member of the crews will grow so bored with the enforced delay in that desolate spot that he will take a book from the library in the Officers' Mess to help pass the time. He will find there a copy of *Conquering the Arctic Ice*, the book in which I described our sledge journey across the pack ice in search of the Unknown Land.

I suppose that Modern Man, lord of the air, will feel as though he were transported back to primeval times, when he reads how 'prehistoric' man struggled on across the appalling ice in search of the land which was not there, and how he saw some of the ice which Modern Man knows so well, lands on and calls 'T1', 'T2', 'T3' or whatever number of T it will be then.

Perhaps he won't read long; it may well bore him and he will lay the book aside, yawn and dismiss machineless antiquity with a shrug of his shoulders, and think that people who could have thought of doing a thing like that, must have been mad.

There may be something in that, and, indeed, I have been told it hundreds of times. Not that it did any good! Sometimes, I may even have thought it myself, though less often now that Modern Man has found and manned floating ice-islands where I sought land. When you look at it properly, that journey of ours in a past so remote as to be almost unreal, was perhaps not so stupid and rash an undertaking as the wise and the cautious once thought it to be.

I, at least, am glad that I made it.